D0879931

QUICK AND EASY CHINESE MEALS IN MINUTES

by

Thomas K. Neill

foulsham
LONDON • NEW YORK • TORONTO • SYDNEY

foulsham

The Publishing House, Bennetts Close,
Cippenham, Berkshire, SL1 5AP, England

Dedication

To my mother, brother and Yvonne

ISBN 0-572-02186-0

Copyright © 1997 W. Foulsham & Co. Ltd

All rights reserved

The Copyright Act prohibits (subject to
certain very limited exceptions) the making of
copies of any copyright work or of a substantial
part of such a work, including the making of
copies by photocopying or similar process.
Written permission to make a copy or copies
must therefore normally be obtained from the
publisher in advance. It is advisable also to consult
the publisher if in any doubt as to the legality of any
copying which is to be undertaken.

Printed in Great Britain by
Cox & Wyman Ltd, Reading, Berkshire

CONTENTS

INTRODUCTION

In the 1960s I spent seven years at boarding school, during which time I cannot honestly say that I and the other pupils were ever well fed. An evening meal of two warmish sausages, a slice of bread, and stewed, milky, over-sweet tea is hardly a gourmet feast. But, when you are hungry you savour every mouthful, and ever since that time my interest in food of all kinds has grown and grown.

I especially love Chinese and Indian food and wouldn't like to have to say which of these two is my favourite. But, if really pressed, I think Chinese food would win because its subtlety, its taste and its appearance are unsurpassable.

My first experience of Chinese food was in the late '60s when I was a student in Manchester. The restaurant - I don't recall there being take-aways at that time - was near Manchester Cathedral and I must say I was greatly impressed by the meal. I had to wait until the late '70s, when local restaurants began to provide the service, for my first taste of Chinese take-away food.

You may think it is beyond you to create the smells, textures and tastes of the dishes you have eaten in Chinese restaurants or from Chinese take-aways but in fact making your own Chinese food is the easiest thing imaginable. You may not end up with authentic Chinese food as served in China, but you will certainly get authentic restaurant food.

By using the suggested ingredients you will be half-way there. Like Chinese chefs, you will need to prepare all vegetables, meats and sauce ingredients in advance and, once cooking begins, you won't have to break off. I rather enjoy the time given to the preparation, knowing that once it is completed then the actual dish will take only minutes to cook.

When preparing a Chinese menu, try to provide two or three different main dishes to give plenty of variety; as cooking takes such a short time some can be kept warm in a low oven while others are being prepared. Any menu can be 'extended' by serving rice, noodles, vegetable dishes or extras such as prawn crackers and spring rolls.

You don't need to buy any special equipment to make Chinese food; saucepans and frying pans (skillets) are perfectly adequate. However, should you feel like buying just one piece of Chinese equipment, I would recommend a wok - it can serve for stir-frying, deep-frying or steaming. Many people enjoy using chopsticks and if you feel you want to, and can handle them, then do so. However, most Chinese restaurants provide a spoon and fork and give chopsticks only if asked.

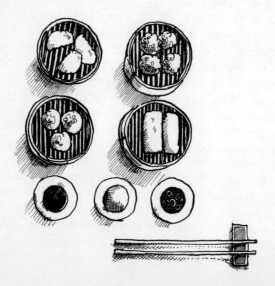

Ingredients & Methods

The main ingredients used in the recipes are to be found in the list below. Also included are some sauces not mentioned in the recipes, any of which can be substituted for the given sauce recipes in this book. Once you get used to cooking Chinese food you will want to experiment to get your own particular taste. Most of the items in the list are stocked by supermarkets, either under manufacturers' brand names or under the supermarket's own label. Anything not readily available there will be obtainable from Chinese shops, grocers and cash and carry stores.

Spices and flavourings
Chopped black beans
Chinese curry powder
Five spice powder
Fresh root ginger
Star anise

Sauces and pastes
Black bean paste
Black bean sauce
Chilli and tomato sauce
Dark soy sauce
Ginger and honey spare rib sauce
Hoisin sauce
Hot chilli sauce
Lemon sauce
Light soy sauce
Orange and sherry spare rib sauce
Orange and honey spare rib sauce
Real oyster sauce
Sweet and sour sauce
Sweet chilli sauce
Yellow bean sauce
Yellow bean paste

Marinades and oil
Chilli and garlic marinade
Classic Chinese marinade
Ginger and spring onion (scallion) marinade
Pure sesame oil

Vegetables
Baby sweetcorn (corn)
Bamboo shoots
Bean sprouts
Dried chinese mushrooms
Tinned straw mushrooms
Water chestnuts

Noodles and rice
Instant noodles
Medium egg noodles
Thread egg noodles
Chinese long grain rice

Miscellaneous
Prawn crackers
Spring roll wrappers
Wonton wrappers

STIR-FRYING

Stir-frying means exactly what it says: the food is fried (sautéed) in oil, over high heat, while you stir it continuously.

Always heat the pan or wok first before adding the oil - that way nothing sticks. Then heat the oil until very hot and finally add the ingredients in the order given in the recipes and stir-fry for the stated times.

Everything cooks quickly and evenly and you have crisp, tasty food cooked at speed.

Cutting Chicken, Meat and Vegetables

In Chinese cooking, all ingredients are cut to more or less the same shape and size. This is done for a number of reasons, the chief one being so they take similar times to cook. They will also look good.

Chicken Breast

I always cut chicken breast very thinly across the grain. Depending on the size of the breast, each slice should end up approximately 5 mm (¹/₄ in) thick by 7.5 cm (3 in). This is how chicken breasts should be prepared for all those recipes that specify 'chicken breast, sliced'.

For most of the recipes you can cube the chicken

instead if you prefer. To do this, cut the breast lengthways into 2.5 cm (1 in) thick strips, then cut each of the strips into 2.5 cm (1 in) cubes.

Meat

Rump steak is the cut I always use for Chinese meat dishes. You can use a more expensive cut if you like but, whichever one you choose, *always* cut across the grain or it will be tough. If you have a largish piece of meat, begin by cutting it into smaller lengths about 5 cm (2 in) wide. Then cut across the grain into slices about 5 mm ($^1/_4$ in) thick by 5 cm (2 in). If using pork, choose lean pork steaks and cut as for rump steak.

Prawns (Shrimp)

In most of the recipes for king prawns (jumbo shrimp) you can substitute thawed frozen prawns.

Fresh king prawns should be prepared before use: remove the shell and, using a very sharp knife, cut along the centre of the back and pull out and discard the vein. Wash the prawns well and then dry.

Cooked prawns will take less time to cook than raw.

Vegetables

For red or green (bell) peppers, cut in half and remove the seeds and the pith-like membrane. Then either slice the halves thinly or cut into halves again, then into quarters and finally into triangular shapes.

For carrots, the easiest and quickest way is to clean and scrape them, slice thinly, then blanch in a pan of simmering water for about 5 minutes. You can blanch in bulk, freeze and use as required.

Dried Chinese Mushrooms

I would strongly advise you to buy some dried mushrooms. They are expensive, but they last for ages and really do add that extra something to Chinese dishes.

To reconstitute, heat about 600 ml/1 pt/$2^1/2$ cups of water in a saucepan and when hot add the required number of dried mushrooms. Leave to soak for 30 minutes. Remove from the pan and squeeze to extract excess water. If the stalks are still attached they should be removed as they are hard and inedible.

Fresh Ginger and Garlic

Fresh ginger is now almost universally available in supermarkets. To prepare garlic and ginger, first peel the clove or piece, then cut into thin slices. Reassemble roughly, cut into slices across the grain, then cut into fine dice. Ginger and garlic can also be crushed.

NOTES ON RECIPES

- All the cooking times given in the book are approximate. Depending on the heat source used, you may have to increase or decrease the time taken for the ingredients to cook. Do remember, though, that vegetables must retain their crunchiness, and should not be cooked until mushy or completely wilted.

- When following a recipe, use either metric, Imperial or American measurements. Never change from one to the other.

- All spoon measurements are level.

- Eggs are medium size unless otherwise stated.

- All recipes are those found on the menu at Chinese restaurants and provide two servings. If you wish to cook for four either double the recipe or cook additional two-serving dishes. Suggestions are given at the end of the book for set menus for two, three and four people.

BASIC RECIPES

Several basic ingredients crop up time and again in Chinese cooking. Make life easier for yourself by making these in bulk and freezing in small portions until you need then. For those who like a Chinese-style curry, a basic sauce is given at the end of this section so you can make your own.

CHICKEN STOCK

Makes about 2 l/3½ pts/8½ cups	Metric	Imperial	American
Chicken, carcass and bones	1	1	1
Fresh root ginger, peeled	2.5 cm piece	1 in piece	1 in piece
Leek, left whole	1 small	1 small	1 small
Garlic cloves, peeled	4	4	4

1. Put the carcass and bones into a large saucepan. Add 2.25 litres/4 pts/10 cups of cold water and bring to the boil. Reduce heat and simmer, uncovered, for 1½ hours.

2. Strain the liquid into a clean pan and discard the carcass and other residue. Cool, then leave in the fridge overnight.

3. Spoon off any fat that has risen to the top, strain the stock through muslin (cheesecloth) or a kitchen cloth and then freeze in suitable sized containers such as yoghurt pots until required.

Preparation time: 10 minutes
Cooking time: 1½ hours, plus chilling

14

WONTON AND SPRING ROLL WRAPPERS

Should you be unable to buy either of these, the following recipes provide an acceptable alternative.

WONTON WRAPPERS

This is basically a pasta recipe, very similar to fresh lasagne.

Serves 2	Metric	Imperial	American
Plain (all-purpose) flour	225 g	8 oz	2 cups
Egg	1	1	1
Cold water	120 ml	4 fl oz	½ cup
Salt	2.5 ml	½ tsp	½ tsp
Cornflour (cornstarch)	30 ml	2 tbsp	2 tbsp

1. Put all the ingredients except the cornflour into a bowl and mix together thoroughly with your hands. Knead for 3 minutes until smooth. Cover the bowl with cling-film (plastic wrap) and leave for 1 hour.

2. Divide the dough into six and roll out each piece as thinly as possible. Cut each into a 10 cm/4 in square. Put the cornflour on a plate and dip each square into it to coat well on both sides, and prevent sticking. Pile the finished squares on top of each other and use as required or freeze for future use.

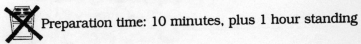 Preparation time: 10 minutes, plus 1 hour standing

SPRING ROLL WRAPPERS

Serves 2	Metric	Imperial	American
Plain (all-purpose) flour	100 g	4 oz	1 cup
Cold water	250 ml	8 fl oz	1 cup
Salt	2.5 ml	½ tsp	½ tsp

1. Mix together all the ingredients in a bowl to form a batter. Cover and leave to stand for 1 hour.

2. Take a medium-sized frying pan (skillet), heat and barely grease it. Pour about 30 ml/2 tbsp of the batter into the hot pan and spread it over the base, as if making a very thin pancake. If there are any tiny holes on the surface, dip your finger in some uncooked batter and use to fill them in.

3. When golden on one side, turn over and cook the other side. When golden, remove from the pan and repeat for the remaining batter.

4. Allow to go cold, then use in recipes or freeze for future use.

Preparation time: 10 minutes, plus 1 hour standing
Cooking time: About 15 minutes

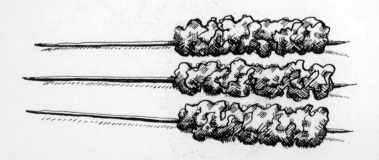

BASIC SAUCES

Preparing these basic sauces in advance will speed up your cooking.

DARK SAUCE

Serves 2	Metric	Imperial	American
Dark soy sauce	*30 ml*	*2 tbsp*	*2 tbsp*
Sherry	*15 ml*	*1 tbsp*	*1 tbsp*
Sugar	*15 ml*	*1 tbsp*	*1 tbsp*
Cornflour (cornstarch)	*10 ml*	*2 tsp*	*2 tsp*
Stock or water	*60 ml*	*4 tbsp*	*4 tbsp*

Mix together all the ingredients and use in the individual recipes where Dark Sauce is called for.

Preparation time: 3 minutes

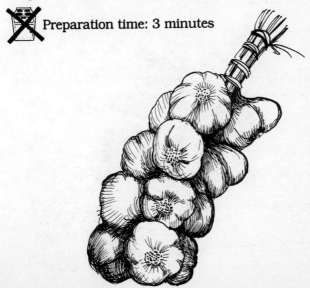

SWEET AND SOUR SAUCE

Serves 2	Metric	Imperial	American
Vinegar	30 ml	2 tbsp	2 tbsp
Sugar	45 ml	3 tbsp	3 tbsp
Pinch of salt			
Tomato ketchup (catsup)	15 ml	1 tbsp	1 tbsp
Light soy sauce	15 ml	1 tbsp	1 tbsp
Cornflour (cornstarch)	15 ml	1 tbsp	1 tbsp
Orange squash, undiluted	15 ml	1 tbsp	1 tbsp
Stock or water	45 ml	3 tbsp	3 tbsp
Pineapple juice	15 ml	1 tbsp	1 tbsp

Mix together all the ingredients and use in the individual recipes where indicated, or serve as an 'extra'.

 Preparation time: 5 minutes

LIGHT SAUCE

Serves 2	Metric	Imperial	American
Light soy sauce	*15 ml*	*1 tbsp*	*1 tbsp*
Sherry	*30 ml*	*2 tbsp*	*2 tbsp*
Water	*15 ml*	*1 tbsp*	*1 tbsp*
Sugar	*10 ml*	*2 tsp*	*2 tsp*
Cornflour (cornstarch)	*5 ml*	*1 tsp*	*1 tsp*

Mix together all the ingredients and use in the individual recipes where Light Sauce is called for.

Preparation time: 5 minutes

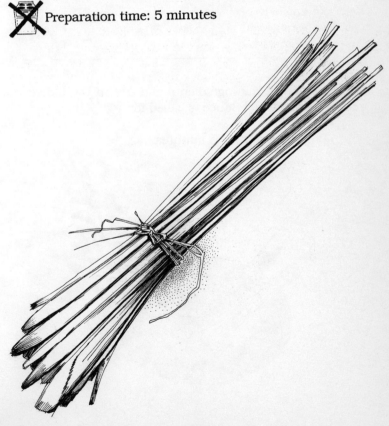

CHILLI SAUCE

Serves 2	Metric	Imperial	American
Finely chopped fresh root ginger	5 ml	1 tsp	1 tsp
Finely chopped spring onion (scallion)	15 ml	1 tbsp	1 tbsp
Stock or water	30 ml	2 tbsp	2 tbsp
Sherry	30 ml	2 tbsp	2 tbsp
Sweet chilli sauce	15 ml	1 tbsp	1 tbsp
Sugar	10 ml	2 tsp	2 tsp
Pinch of salt			
Vinegar	5 ml	1 tsp	1 tsp
Pinch of five spice powder			
Cornflour (cornstarch)	5 ml	1 tsp	1 tsp
Water	5 ml	1 tsp	1 tsp

Mix together all the ingredients and use in the individual recipes where Chilli Sauce is called for.

 Preparation time: 5 minutes

SATAY SAUCE

Serves 2	Metric	Imperial	American
Smooth peanut butter	15 ml	1 tbsp	1 tbsp
Cold water	30 ml	2 tbsp	2 tbsp
Light soy sauce	30 ml	2 tbsp	2 tbsp
Finely chopped spring onion (scallion), green only	30 ml	2 tbsp	2 tbsp
Lemon juice	5 ml	1 tsp	1 tsp
Sugar	10 ml	2 tsp	2 tsp
Pinch of ground ginger			
Garlic purée	5 ml	1 tsp	1 tsp
Pinch of chilli powder			
Honey	5 ml	1 tsp	1 tsp

Mix together all the ingredients and use in the individual recipes where Satay Sauce is called for.

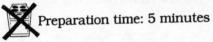 Preparation time: 5 minutes

TOMATO SAUCE

Serves 2	Metric	Imperial	American
Red wine vinegar	45 ml	3 tbsp	3 tbsp
Sugar	45 ml	3 tbsp	3 tbsp
Cornflour (cornstarch)	5 ml	1 tsp	1 tsp
Water	5 ml	1 tsp	1 tsp
Tomato ketchup (catsup)	15 ml	1 tbsp	1 tbsp

Mix together all the ingredients and use in the individual recipes where Tomato Sauce is called for.

 Preparation time: 5 minutes

PRAWN CRACKERS

These are readily available in supermarkets either raw or ready-cooked. When raw they are quite small and hard but grow considerably when deep fried, and have a crunchy texture. The ready-cooked versions sometimes have a better texture and are certainly quick and easy – just open the pack.

PRECOOKED CHICKEN

I specify raw chicken breast in most of the recipes, but skinned then precooked chicken portions can be used instead.

Serves 2	Metric	Imperial	American
Chicken portions	900 g	2 lb	2 lb
Five spice powder	5 ml	1 tsp	1 tsp
Garlic cloves	2	2	2
Roughly chopped fresh root ginger	5 ml	1 tsp	1 tsp
Cold water	1.2 litres	2 pts	5 cups

Place everything in a saucepan and cook for approximately 45 minutes until the chicken is tender. Drain well, cool, and freeze in 225 g/8 oz portions if not using immediately.

For use in soups, it is a good idea to precook two chicken breasts. To do this, cut each breast into four, place in a saucepan and add 600 ml/1 pt/2½ cups of water. Bring to the boil and simmer, uncovered, for about 30 minutes until tender. Allow to cool, then chop very finely or mince. Divide into 50 g/2 oz portions, wrap in clingfilm (plastic wrap) and freeze until required.

Preparation time: 5 minutes
Cooking time: 45 minutes

PRECOOKED BEEF

Follow the recipe for Precooked Chicken but substitute the same quantity of cubed beef for the chicken and cook for up to 60 minutes until tender.

For use in soups, I always have some precooked minced (ground) beef available. To do this, place 225 g/8 oz/2 cups of mince in a saucepan with 600 ml/1 pt/2½ cups of water. Bring to the boil and simmer for about 30 minutes until tender. Pour the mince and water into a bowl and leave to go cold, then place in the fridge or freezer for about 30 minutes. At the end of this time remove the fat, which will have risen to the surface and hardened. Drain the mince thoroughly and divide into 50 g/2 oz/½ cups portions. Place in clingfilm (plastic wrap) and freeze until required.

PRECOOKED PORK

Follow the recipe for Precooked Chicken but substitute the same quantity of lean cubed pork for the chicken and cook for up to 60 minutes until tender.

PRECOOKED DUCK

For all the recipes using chicken you can use duck breast or portions, which can be bought in most supermarkets. If using portions, skin them and remove any excess fat. Use duck breast exactly as you would chicken breast.

For precooked duck, divide each portion into three and follow the recipe for Precooked Chicken.

PRECOOKED RICE

Rice can be precooked in bulk and kept in 175 g/6 oz/1½ cups (cooked weight) portions in the freezer to be used in various fried rice dishes.

CHINESE CURRIES

If you like Chinese curries you can make them with the following recipes, and include onions, diced meat or prawns (shrimp) and vegetables such as potatoes, carrots, mushrooms and peas.

CURRY SAUCE

Serves 2	Metric	Imperial	American
Chinese curry powder	15 ml	1 tbsp	1 tbsp
Oil	45ml	3 tbsp	3 tbsp
Onion, thinly sliced	50 g	2 oz	$1/2$ cup
Onion Purée (page 26)	75ml	5 tbsp	5 tbsp
Sugar	5 ml	1 tsp	1 tsp
Star anise	$1/2$	$1/2$	$1/2$
Stock	50ml	2 fl oz	$3^n/2$ tbsp

1. Mix the curry powder to a paste in a cup with 30 ml/ 2 tbsp of water.

2. Heat the oil and fry (sauté) the onion until soft but not browned. Add the Onion Purée, sugar, star anise, stock and curry powder mixture and cook for about 10 minutes. Use in individual recipes where indicated. or serve as a side dish.

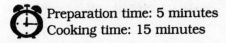
Preparation time: 5 minutes
Cooking time: 15 minutes

Onion Purée

This recipe for onion purée is used when making Chinese curries. It gives a typical take-away style sauce. It can be made up in larger quantities and when cold frozen in cream or yoghurt pots for future use.

Serves 2	Metric	Imperial	American
Peeled and roughly chopped onion	*225 g*	*8 oz*	*2 cups*
Cold water	*600 ml*	*1 pt*	*2½ cups*

1. Put the onion and water in a saucepan and bring to the boil.

2. Reduce to a strong simmer and cook for about 30 minutes. Drain.

3. Blend or process the onion for about 1 minute until really smooth. Use in recipe or freeze for future use.

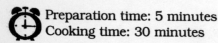 Preparation time: 5 minutes
Cooking time: 30 minutes

Chinese Curry Powder

You can buy Chinese curry powder or you can make your own by adding 15 ml/1 tbsp of five spice powder to 105 ml/7 tbsp of ordinary curry powder. Mix together thoroughly and store in a jar.

STARTERS

This selection of starters will be familiar from any good Chinese menu. They are surprisingly easy to prepare and will really whet your appetite for the more filling main course dishes to follow.

PEKING-STYLE SPARE RIBS

Serves 2	Metric	Imperial	American
Pork spare ribs	900 g	2 lb	2 lb
Brown sugar	105 g	7 tbsp	7 tbsp
Dark soy sauce	105 g	7 tbsp	7 tbsp
Spring onions (scallions), left whole	3	3	3
Piece of fresh root ginger	5 cm square	2 in square	2 in square
Sherry	60 ml	4 tbsp	4 tbsp
Small pinch of five spice powder			

1. Divide the spare ribs into individual ribs by cutting between them. Put them into a large saucepan and add all the other ingredients and 1.2 litres/2 pts/5 cups of cold water. Bring to the boil and cook over medium heat for about 45 minutes. Stir well every 20 minutes or so.

2. Remove and discard the spring onion and ginger. Continue to cook over a high heat for about 15 minutes until the liquid thickens and coats the ribs. Serve hot or allow to go cold and freeze until required.

 Preparation time: 10 minutes
Cooking time: 1 hour

CHILLI SPARE RIBS

Serves 2	Metric	Imperial	American
Pork spare ribs	900 g	2 lb	2 lb
Oil for deep frying			
For the sauce			
Dark soy sauce	30 ml	2 tbsp	2 tbsp
Sherry	50 ml	2 fl oz	3½ tbsp
Hoisin sauce	30 ml	2 tbsp	2 tbsp
Yellow bean paste	15 ml	1 tbsp	1 tbsp
Crushed garlic	10 ml	2 tsp	2 tsp
Brown sugar	10 ml	2 tsp	2 tsp
Sweet chilli sauce	15 ml	1 tbsp	1 tbsp
Spring onions (scallions), chopped	2	2	2

1. Divide the spare ribs into individual ribs by cutting between them. Heat the oil and deep-fry the ribs until the meat shrinks away from the bone and is crisp and golden brown. Drain well on kitchen paper.

2. Mix together all the sauce ingredients in a large saucepan and bring to the boil.

3. Add the cooked spare ribs and simmer gently for about 35 minutes until really tender. Remove from the sauce.

4. Serve hot, or allow to go cold and freeze until required.

Preparation time: 10 minutes
Cooking time: 45 minutes

BARBECUED SPARE RIBS

Serves 2	Metric	Imperial	American
Pork spare ribs	*900 g*	*2 lb*	*2 lb*
For the sauce			
Brown sugar	*30 ml*	*2 tbsp*	*2 tbsp*
Tomato ketchup (catsup)	*30 ml*	*2 tbsp*	*2 tbsp*
Hoisin sauce	*15 ml*	*1 tbsp*	*1 tbsp*
Worcestershire sauce	*15 ml*	*1 tbsp*	*1 tbsp*
Red wine vinegar	*30 ml*	*2 tbsp*	*2 tbsp*
Honey	*30 ml*	*2 tbsp*	*2 tbsp*

1. Divide the spare ribs into individual ribs by cutting between them. Heat the oil and deep-fry the ribs until the meat shrinks away from the bone and is crisp and golden brown. Drain well on kitchen paper.

2. Mix together all the sauce ingredients.

3. Place the cooked ribs in a large, flat ovenproof dish and pour the sauce over them.

4. Place in an oven preheated to 190°C/375°F/gas mark 5 for about 40 minutes, basting now and again. If, at the end of this time, the sauce is not thick and syrupy in consistency, pour off into a saucepan and boil until reduced, then pour over the hot ribs.

 Preparation time: 10 minutes
Cooking time: 45 minutes

DEEP-FRIED WONTONS WITH SWEET AND SOUR SAUCE

Serves 2	Metric	Imperial	American
Wonton wrappers	20	20	20
Oil for deep frying			
Sweet and Sour Sauce (page 18) 1 recipe			
For the filling			
Chicken or pork, minced	100 g	4 oz	1 cup
Prawns (shrimp), minced	25 g	1 oz	2 tbsp
Sugar	5 ml	1 tsp	1 tsp
Salt	5 ml	1 tsp	1 tsp
Spring onion (scallion), finely chopped	1	1	1
Light soy sauce	15 ml	1 tbsp	1 tbsp
Pinch of five spice powder			

1. Place the filling ingredients in a bowl and mix thoroughly with your hands.

2. Take a wonton wrapper and place 5 ml/1 tsp of the filling in the centre. With your finger, dab water around the outside edges of the wrapper, then gather up the corners, press and twist closed to make a little bag. Repeat until all the filling is used up.

3. Heat the oil and add the wontons. Cook over a medium heat for about 2 minutes until they are golden. Remove and drain on paper towel.

4. Heat the sauce in a pan until it comes to the boil and has thickened a little. Pour over the fried wontons and serve.

Preparation time: 15–20 minutes
Cooking time: 4 minutes

SPRING ROLLS

Serves 2	Metric	Imperial	American
Oil	30 ml	2 tbsp	2 tbsp
Chicken or pork, finely chopped	100 g	4 oz	1 cup
Spring onion (scallion), finely chopped	1	1	1
Button mushrooms, finely chopped	50 g	2 oz	4 tbsp
Finely chopped celery	50 g	2 oz	4 tbsp
Cornflour (cornstarch)	7.5 ml	1½ tsp	1½ tsp
Dark soy sauce	15 ml	1 tbsp	1 tbsp
Sugar	5 ml	1 tsp	1 tsp
Plain (all-purpose) flour	15 ml	1 tbsp	1 tbsp
Spring roll wrappers	8	8	8
Oil for deep-frying			

1. Heat the oil, add the meat and fry (sauté) until golden.

2. Add the vegetables and stir-fry for 2 minutes.

3. Mix the cornflour with 22.5 ml/1½ tbsp of cold water and add to the meat with the soy sauce, sugar and vegetables. Stir until thickened. Season to taste. Allow to go cold.

4. To make the paste, mix the flour with 15 ml/1 tbsp of cold water.

5. To fill the rolls, place about 25 g/1 oz/2 tbsp of the filling in a strip 5 cm/2 in in from each side and the base of the wrapper. Fold the unfilled piece at the base over to cover the filling. Fold the unfilled right side over the filling towards the left and the unfilled left side over the filling towards the right. Now roll up tightly and seal the join of the roll with the flour and water paste.

6. Deep-fry the prepared spring rolls in oil heated to 180°C/350°F for about 5 minutes until golden brown.

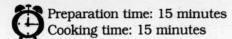
Preparation time: 15 minutes
Cooking time: 15 minutes

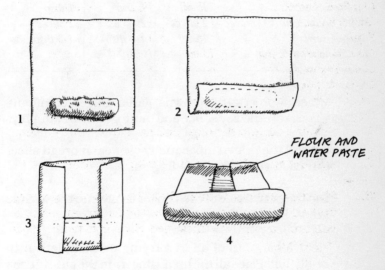

FLOUR AND WATER PASTE

Prawn Toast

Serves 2	Metric	Imperial	American
Prawns (shrimp), thawed if frozen	100 g	4 oz	1 cup
Finely chopped garlic	5 ml	1 tsp	1 tsp
Finely chopped fresh root ginger	5 ml	1 tsp	1 tsp
Cornflour (cornstarch)	5 ml	1 tsp	1 tsp
Sugar	5 ml	1 tsp	1 tsp
Pinch of salt			
Light soy sauce	15 ml	1 tbsp	1 tbsp
White bread, crusts removed	2 slices	2 slices	2 slices
Sesame seeds	15-30 ml	1-2 tbsp	1-2 tbsp
Oil for shallow frying			

1. Mince or process the prawns, garlic, ginger, cornflour, sugar, salt and soy sauce and mix together thoroughly.

2. Spread the prawn mix equally over each bread slice. Cut each slice into three fingers.

3. Dip the prawn side of each finger firmly into the sesame seeds.

4. Heat 5 cm/2 in of oil in a frying pan (skillet) until really hot. Place all the bread fingers in the oil and cook for about 2–3 minutes on both sides until golden.

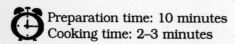

Preparation time: 10 minutes
Cooking time: 2–3 minutes

MARBLED TEA EGGS

Serves 2	Metric	Imperial	American
Eggs, at room temperature	2	2	2
Pinch of salt			
Star anise	2	2	2
Dark soy sauce	45 ml	3 tbsp	3 tbsp
Five spice powder	10 ml	2 tsp	2 tsp
Tea-leaves or	10 ml	2 tsp	2tsp
tea-bag	1	1	1
Brown sugar	5 ml	1 tsp	1 tsp

1. Place the eggs in a saucepan and add about 300ml/½ pt/ 1¼ cups of cold water, so they are just covered. Cook for about 10 minutes until hard-boiled (hard-cooked). Take the eggs from the pan, leaving the water behind. Leave the eggs to go cold or run them under cold water to speed cooling.

2. Gently tap the eggs all over with a teaspoon to give a crazy-paving effect.

3. Mix together all the other ingredients and add to the reserved water in the pan.

4. Return the eggs to the pan and boil for about 30 minutes over medium heat. Turn off the heat and leave the eggs in the liquid overnight.

5. When ready to use, remove the shells. The crazy-paving effect should now be transferred to the egg white.

 Preparation time: 5 minutes
Cooking time: 40 minutes, plus standing

Prawn-stuffed Mushrooms

Serves 2	Metric	Imperial	American
Prawns (shrimp), thawed if frozen	100 g	4 oz	1 cup
Finely chopped garlic	5 ml	1 tsp	1 tsp
Finely chopped fresh root ginger	5 ml	1 tsp	1 tsp
Cornflour (cornstarch)	5 ml	1 tsp	1 tsp
Sugar	5 ml	1 tsp	1 tsp
Pinch of salt			
Light soy sauce	15 ml	1 tbsp	1 tbsp
Spring onion (scallion), green part only, very finely chopped	1	1	1
Large button mushrooms	10	10	10
Sesame seeds	15-30 ml	1-2 tbsp	1-2 tbsp
Oil for deep frying			

1. Mince or process the prawns, garlic, ginger, cornflour, sugar, salt, soy sauce and spring onion and mix together thoroughly.

2. Stuff the mushrooms with the mixture, then dip each paste-side down into the sesame seeds.

3. Heat the oil and deep-fry the mushrooms for 2–3 minutes.

Preparation time: 10 minutes
Cooking time: 2–3 minutes

Soups

Chinese soups tend to be thinner and less substantial than conventional soups. They are nevertheless full of flavour and set the mood for the rest of the meal.

HOT AND SOUR SOUP

Serves 2	Metric	Imperial	American
Oil	*15 ml*	*1 tbsp*	*1 tbsp*
Dried Chinese mushrooms, reconstituted and sliced	*4*	*4*	*4*
Sherry or orange juice	*15 ml*	*1 tbsp*	*1 tbsp*
Light soy sauce	*15 ml*	*1 tbsp*	*1 tbsp*
Sugar	*15 ml*	*1 tbsp*	*1 tbsp*
Red wine vinegar	*15 ml*	*1 tbsp*	*1 tbsp*
Precooked Chicken (page 23), finely chopped	*50 g*	*2 oz*	*1½ cups*
Stock	*600 ml*	*1 pt*	*2½ cups*
Spring onion (scallion), green part only, finely chopped	*1*	*1*	*1*

1. Heat the oil in a saucepan and stir-fry the mushrooms for 1 minute.

2. Add the sherry or orange juice, soy sauce, sugar, red wine vinegar, chicken and stock. Stir well and heat through.

3. Finally, add the spring onion and serve in bowls.

Preparation time: 5 minutes
Cooking time: 5 minutes

WEST LAKE SOUP

Serves 2	Metric	Imperial	American
Sesame oil	10 ml	2 tsp	2 tsp
Precooked Mince (page 24)	50 g	2 oz	½ cup
Finely chopped garlic	5 ml	1 tsp	1 tsp
Finely chopped fresh root ginger	5 ml	1 tsp	1 tsp
Cornflour (cornstarch)	15 ml	1 tbsp	1 tbsp
Stock	600 ml	1 pt	2½ cups
Red wine vinegar	10 ml	2 tsp	2 tsp
Sugar	5 ml	1 tsp	1 tsp
Tinned straw mushrooms	50 g	2 oz	¼ cup
Finely chopped spring onion (scallion)	10 ml	2 tsp	2 tsp
Egg white	1	1	1

1. Heat the oil, add the mince and stir-fry for 1 minute.

2. Add the garlic and ginger and fry for 1 minute.

3. Mix the cornflour with 30 ml/2 tbsp of cold water and add to the mince with the stock, red wine vinegar, sugar, straw mushrooms and spring onion. Heat through until thickened slightly. Turn off heat.

4. Beat the egg white and, in a steady stream, pour into the soup. Stir gently, then serve.

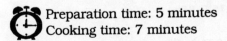
Preparation time: 5 minutes
Cooking time: 7 minutes

CHICKEN AND SWEETCORN SOUP

Serves 2	Metric	Imperial	American
Oil	15 ml	1 tbsp	1 tbsp
Tinned sweetcorn (corn), drained	30 ml	2 tbsp	2 tbsp
Cornflour (cornstarch)	15 ml	1 tbsp	1 tbsp
Chicken stock	600 ml	1 pt	2½ cups
Salt	2.5 ml	½ tsp	½ tsp
Egg white	1	1	1
Precooked Chicken (page 23), very finely chopped or minced	50 g	2 oz	½ cup
Spring onion (scallion), green part only, finely chopped	10 ml	2 tsp	2 tsp

1. Heat the oil and stir-fry the sweetcorn for 30 seconds.

2. Mix the cornflour with 30 ml/2 tbsp of cold water and add to the sweetcorn with the stock and salt. Heat until thickened slightly. Turn off the heat.

3. Beat the egg white and, in a thin stream, pour it into the soup. Stir gently until a ribbon effect appears.

4. Divide the chicken between two bowls and pour the soup on top. Finally, sprinkle the spring onion over the soup.

 Preparation time: 5 minutes
Cooking time: 5 minutes

Crabmeat and Sweetcorn Soup

Follow the recipe for Sweetcorn and Chicken Soup but substitute 50 g/2 oz/¹/₂ cup of finely chopped crabmeat for the chicken.

CHICKEN AND MUSHROOM SOUP

Serves 2	Metric	Imperial	American
Oil	15 ml	1 tbsp	1 tbsp
Button mushrooms, thinly sliced	50 g	2 oz	1 cup
Finely chopped fresh root ginger	5 ml	1 tsp	1 tsp
Finely chopped garlic	5 ml	1 tsp	1 tsp
Cornflour (cornstarch)	15 ml	1 tbsp	1 tbsp
Stock	600 ml	1 pt	2½ cups
Sesame oil	5 ml	1 tsp	1 tsp
Spring onion (scallion), finely chopped	1	1	1
Precooked Chicken (page 23), very finely chopped or minced	50 g	2 oz	½ cup

1. Heat the cooking oil, add the sliced mushrooms and stir-fry for 3 minutes.

2. Add the ginger and garlic and stir-fry for 1 minute.

3. Mix the cornflour with 30 ml/2 tbsp of cold water and add to the mushrooms with the remaining ingredients. Heat through until thickened slightly. Serve.

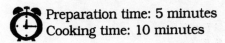 Preparation time: 5 minutes
Cooking time: 10 minutes

Main Dishes

Choose two or more main dishes with the extras of your choice for a really satisfying meal. Experiment with tastes and textures and have fun deciding which combinations suit your personal palate.

CHICKEN WITH MUSHROOMS

Serves 2	Metric	Imperial	American
Chicken breast, sliced	225 g	8 oz	2 cups
Cornflour (cornstarch)	5 ml	1 tsp	1 tsp
Oil	45 ml	3 tbsp	3 tbsp
Button mushrooms, halved	100 g	4 oz	2 cups
Thinly sliced carrot, blanched	25 g	1 oz	¼ cup
Dried Chinese mushrooms, reconstituted and thinly sliced	5	5	5
Roughly chopped onion	50 g	2 oz	½ cup
Bean sprouts	25 g	1 oz	¼ cup
Crushed garlic	5 ml	1 tsp	1 tsp
Crushed fresh root ginger	5 ml	1 tsp	1 tsp
Dark Sauce (page 17) 1 recipe			

1. Mix the cornflour with 10 ml/2 tsp of water and place in a bowl with the chicken. Stir to coat thoroughly. Leave to marinate for about 15 minutes.

2. Heat the oil, add the chicken and stir-fry for about 3 minutes until just tender.

3. Add the button mushrooms, carrot, Chinese mushrooms, onion, bean sprouts, garlic and ginger and stir-fry for 2-3 minutes.

4. Finally, add the sauce and stir until the sauce has thickened slightly and is heated through.

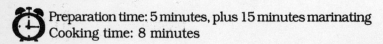 Preparation time: 5 minutes, plus 15 minutes marinating
Cooking time: 8 minutes

Beef with Mushrooms

Follow the recipe for Chicken with Mushrooms but substitute 225 g/8 oz/2 cups of sliced beef for the chicken. Add 15 ml/ 1 tbsp of finely chopped spring onions (scallion) at step 4.

Pork with Mushrooms

Follow the recipe for Chicken with Mushrooms but substitute 225 g/8 oz/2 cups of sliced pork for the chicken and cook for 5 minutes. Add a quartered tomato at step 3.

Prawns with Mushrooms

Follow the recipe for Chicken with Mushrooms but substitute 225 g/8 oz/2 cups of thawed prawns (shrimp) for the chicken and cook for 2 minutes. Add 15 ml/1 tbsp finely chopped fresh coriander (cilantro) at step 4.

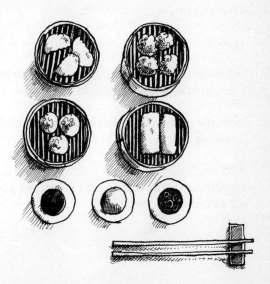

CHICKEN WITH CASHEW NUTS

Serves 2	Metric	Imperial	American
Chicken breast, sliced	225 g	8 oz	2 cups
Cornflour (cornstarch)	5 ml	1 tsp	1 tsp
Oil	45 ml	3 tbsp	3 tbsp
Cashew nuts	50 g	2 oz	½ cup
Roughly chopped onion	50 g	2 oz	½ cup
Crushed garlic	10 ml	2 tsp	2 tsp
Finely chopped fresh root ginger	5 ml	1 tsp	1 tsp
Sliced carrot, blanched	25 g	1 oz	2 tbsp
Button mushrooms, sliced	25 g	1 oz	½ cup
Tinned pineapple ring, cut into 8 chunks	1	1	1
Small green (bell) pepper, sliced	½	½	½
Chilli Sauce (page 20) 1 recipe			
Pineapple juice	30 ml	2 tbsp	2 tbsp
Chopped fresh coriander (cilantro)	15 ml	1 tbsp	1 tbsp

1. Marinate the chicken in the cornflour mixed with 5 ml/ 1 tsp of cold water for about 15 minutes.

2. Heat the oil, add the chicken and cook for about 3 minutes until tender.

3. Add the cashew nuts, onion, garlic, ginger, carrot, mushrooms, pineapple and green pepper and stir-fry for about 3 minutes.

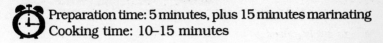

4. Add the sauce and pineapple juice and heat through over a high heat until slightly thickened. Serve sprinkled with the coriander.

Preparation time: 5 minutes, plus 15 minutes marinating
Cooking time: 10–15 minutes

Beef with Cashew Nuts

Follow the recipe for Chicken with Cashew Nuts but substitute 225 g/8 oz/2 cups of sliced beef for the chicken at step 1 and substitute 50 g/2 oz/^{1}/$_2$ cup of chopped green beans for the green (bell) pepper.

Pork with Cashew Nuts

Follow the recipe for Chicken with Cashew Nuts but substitute 225 g/8 oz/2 cups of sliced pork for the chicken.

PRAWNS WITH CASHEW NUTS

Serves 2	Metric	Imperial	American
Tomato ketchup (catsup)	15 ml	1 tbsp	1 tbsp
Dark soy sauce	15 ml	1 tbsp	1 tbsp
Sugar	5 ml	1 tsp	1 tsp
Oil	30 ml	2 tbsp	2 tbsp
Crushed fresh root ginger	5 ml	1 tsp	1 tsp
Crushed garlic	5 ml	1 tsp	1 tsp
Prawns (shrimp), thawed if frozen	225 g	8 oz	2 cups
Cornflour (cornstarch)	5 ml	1 tsp	1 tsp
Cashew nuts	50 g	2 oz	½ cup
Worcestershire sauce	10 ml	2 tsp	2 tsp
Sweet chilli sauce	10 ml	2 tsp	2 tsp
Vinegar	10 ml	2 tsp	2 tsp
Spring onion (scallion), finely chopped	1	1	1

1. Mix together the tomato ketchup, soy sauce and sugar.

2. Heat the oil and stir-fry the ginger and garlic for 1 minute without browning.

3. Add the prawns and cook for about 3 minutes until pink and firm, then add the tomato ketchup and soy sauce mixture. Cook for 30 seconds.

4. Mix the cornflour with 30 ml/2 tbsp of cold water and add to the prawns with the cashew nuts, Worcestershire sauce, chilli sauce and vinegar. Cook for 1 minute.

5. Finally, add the spring onion and serve.

Preparation time: 10 minutes
Cooking time: 7 minutes

CHICKEN SATAY

Serves 2	Metric	Imperial	American
Chicken breast, sliced	225 g	8 oz	2 cups
For the marinade			
Light soy sauce	45 ml	3 tbsp	3 tbsp
Oil	15 ml	1 tbsp	1 tbsp
Smooth peanut butter	15 ml	1 tbsp	1 tbsp
Crushed fresh root ginger	5 ml	1 tsp	1 tsp
Crushed garlic	5 ml	1 tsp	1 tsp
Five spice powder	2.5 ml	½ tsp	½ tsp
Ground cinnamon	2.5 ml	½ tsp	½ tsp
Sugar	5 ml	1 tsp	1 tsp
For dipping			
Curry Sauce (see page 25)			

1. Place the sliced chicken in a dish.

2. Mix together all the marinade ingredients and pour over the chicken. Rub well in using your hands and leave to marinate for up to 24 hours.

3. Soak two bamboo skewers in water, or use the metal variety.

4. Preheat the grill (broiler).

5. Divide the chicken and thread half on to each skewer, spreading it out along the length. Grill (broil) for about 5 minutes, turning once or twice. Serve separately with Curry Sauce as a dipping sauce.

 Preparation time: 10 minutes, plus up to 24 hours marinating
Cooking time: 5 minutes

BEEF SATAY

Serves 2	Metric	Imperial	American
Beef, sliced	225 g	8 oz	2 cups
For the marinade			
Light soy sauce	30 ml	2 tbsp	2 tbsp
Oil	15 ml	1 tbsp	1 tbsp
Smooth peanut butter	15 ml	1 tbsp	1 tbsp
Large pinch of chinese curry powder			
Crushed fresh root ginger	5 ml	1 tsp	1 tsp
Crushed garlic	10 ml	2 tsp	2 tsp
Pinch of five spice powder			
Pinch of ground cinnamon			
Sugar	5 ml	1 tsp	1 tsp

Follow the method for Chicken Satay, using the above marinade at step 2.

 Preparation time: 10 minutes, plus up to 24 hours marinating
Cooking time: 5 minutes

Pork Satay

Follow the recipe for Chicken Satay but substitute 225 g/8 oz/2 cups of sliced pork for the chicken.

PRAWN SATAY

Serves 2	Metric	Imperial	American
Oil	30 ml	2 tbsp	2 tbsp
Crushed garlic	5 ml	1 tsp	1 tsp
Crushed fresh root ginger	5 ml	1 tsp	1 tsp
Prawns (shrimp), thawed if frozen	225 g	8 oz	2 cups
Smooth peanut butter	10 ml	2 tsp	2 tsp
Chilli Sauce (page 20) 1 recipe			
Lettuce leaves	6	6	6

1. Heat the oil and stir-fry the garlic and ginger for 30 seconds. Add the prawns and stir-fry for about a further 3 minutes.

2. Add the peanut butter and the sauce. Heat through until slightly thickened.

3. Just before serving, shred the lettuce leaves and divide between two plates. Place the prawn satay on top.

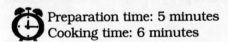 Preparation time: 5 minutes
Cooking time: 6 minutes

CHICKEN WITH PEPPERS AND BLACK BEAN SAUCE

Serves 2	Metric	Imperial	American
Chicken breast, sliced	225 g	8 oz	2 cups
Cornflour (cornstarch)	10 ml	2 tsp	2 tsp
Oil	45 ml	3 tbsp	3 tbsp
Crushed garlic	10 ml	2 tsp	2 tsp
Green (bell) pepper, cut into triangles	100 g	4 oz	4 oz
Roughly chopped onion	50 g	2 oz	½ cup
Black bean sauce	15 ml	1 tbsp	1 tbsp
Light Sauce (page 19) 1 recipe			

1. Marinate the sliced chicken in the cornflour mixed with 10 ml/2 tsp of cold water for about 15 minutes.

2. Heat the oil, add the chicken and cook for 3-5 minutes until tender.

3. Add the garlic, green pepper, onion and black bean sauce and fry for 1 minute.

4. Finally, add the sauce and heat over high heat until slightly thickened.

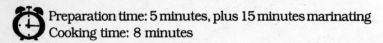 Preparation time: 5 minutes, plus 15 minutes marinating
Cooking time: 8 minutes

Beef with Peppers and Black Bean Sauce

Follow the recipe for Chicken with Peppers and Black Bean Sauce but substitute 225 g/8 oz/2 cups of sliced beef for the chicken.

Pork with Peppers and Black Bean Sauce

Follow the recipe for Chicken with Peppers and Black Bean Sauce but substitute 225 g/8 oz/2 cups of sliced pork for the chicken.

Prawns with Peppers and Black Bean Sauce

Follow the recipe for Chicken with Peppers and Black Bean Sauce but substitute 225 g/8 oz/2 cups of thawed prawns (shrimp) for the chicken. Add 5 ml/1 tsp of crushed fresh root ginger at step 3 and sprinkle 15 ml/1 tbsp of finely chopped spring onion (scallion), green part only, over the dish when serving.

STIR-FRIED CHICKEN WITH ONIONS

Serves 2	Metric	Imperial	American
Cornflour (cornstarch)	5 ml	1 tsp	1 tsp
Chicken breast, sliced	225 g	8 oz	2 cups
Oil	60 ml	4 tbsp	4 tbsp
Onions, halved and thinly sliced	225 g	8 oz	2 cups
Sugar	15 ml	1 tbsp	1 tbsp
Dark soy sauce	15 ml	1 tbsp	1 tbsp
Light soy sauce	15 ml	1 tbsp	1 tbsp

1. Mix the cornflour with 5 ml/1 tsp of cold water and marinate the chicken in this mixture for about 15 minutes.

2. Heat the oil in a frying pan (skillet) and stir-fry the onions until soft and golden.

3. Add the chicken and stir-fry for about 3 minutes.

4. Add the sugar, soy sauces and 15 ml/1 tbsp of cold water. Stir-fry until the sauce has heated through and thickened slightly.

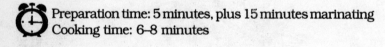 Preparation time: 5 minutes, plus 15 minutes marinating
Cooking time: 6–8 minutes

Stir-fried Beef with Onions

Follow the recipe for Stir-fried Chicken with Onions but substitute 225 g/8 oz/2 cups of sliced beef for the chicken.

Stir-fried Pork with Onions

Follow the recipe for Stir-fried Chicken with Onions but substitute 225 g/8 oz/2 cups sliced pork for the chicken.

Stir-fried Prawns with Onions

Follow the recipe for Stir-fried Chicken with Onions but substitute 225 g/8 oz/2 cups of prawns (shrimp) for the chicken.

SWEET AND SOUR CHICKEN

You can, if you like, prepare and deep-fry double the amount of chicken in batter, and freeze half for use at another time.

Serves 2	Metric	Imperial	American
Chicken breast	225 g	8 oz	8 oz
Whisky	30 ml	2 tbsp	2 tbsp
Brown sugar	10 ml	2 tsp	2 tsp
Light soy sauce	10 ml	2 tsp	2 tsp
Cornflour (cornstarch)	90 ml	6 tbsp	6 tbsp
Oil for deep frying, plus	30 ml	2 tbsp	2 tbsp
Crushed garlic	2.5 ml	1/2 tsp	1/2 tsp
Crushed fresh root ginger	2.5 ml	1/2 tsp	1/2 tsp
Roughly chopped onion	25 g	1 oz	1/4 cup
Thinly sliced carrot, blanched	15 g	1/2 oz	1 tbsp
Green (bell) pepper, cut into triangles	50 g	2 oz	4 tbsp
Tinned pineapple ring, cut into 8 chunks	1	1	1
Pinch of red food colouring powder			
Sweet and Sour Sauce (page 18) 1 recipe			

1. Cut the chicken into pieces approximately 5 x 2.5 cm/ 2 x 1 in and place in a bowl with the whisky, sugar, soy sauce and 10 ml/2 tsp of the cornflour. Mix well and leave for about 30 minutes.

2. Add 15-20 ml/3-4 tsp of cornflour to give a thickish batter which just coats the chicken.

3. Place the remaining cornflour on a plate and, with one hand, lift pieces of chicken with as much batter as possible and quickly transfer to the plate. Roll in the dry cornflour, then remove and place on a clean plate. Repeat until all the chicken has been used up. Allow to sit for about 5 minutes before frying.

4. Heat the oil for deep-frying and add the battered chicken. Cook for about 4 minutes over medium heat until golden and cooked through. Remove and drain.

5. Heat the 30 ml/2 tbsp of oil in a pan, add the garlic and ginger and stir-fry for 30 seconds. Add the onion, carrot and green pepper and stir-fry for 2 minutes. Add the pineapple and fry for 1 minute.

6. Add the sauce and food colouring and heat through until thickened slightly.

7. Reheat the deep-frying oil until very hot, then refry (sauté) the chicken for about 2 minutes. Drain well and add to the saucepan with the sauce mix. Stir well to coat the chicken with the sauce.

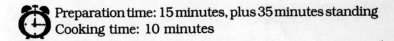 Preparation time: 15 minutes, plus 35 minutes standing
Cooking time: 10 minutes

Sweet and Sour Pork

Follow the recipe for Sweet and Sour Chicken, but substitute 225 g/8 oz/2 cups of cubed pork for the chicken.

SWEET AND SOUR BEEF

Unlike the recipes for Sweet and Sour Chicken and Pork, this recipe does not use batter to coat the beef for deep-frying.

Serves 2	Metric	Imperial	American
Beef	225 g	8 oz	2 cups
Whisky	30 ml	2 tbsp	2 tbsp
Brown sugar	10 ml	2 tsp	2 tsp
Light soy sauce	10 ml	2 tsp	2 tsp
Oil	30 ml	2 tbsp	2 tbsp
Crushed garlic	2.5 ml	1/2 tsp	1/2 tsp
Crushed fresh root ginger	2.5 ml	1/2 tsp	1/2 tsp
Roughly chopped onion	25 g	1 oz	1 tbsp
Thinly sliced carrot, blanched	15 g	1/2 oz	2 tsp
Green (bell) pepper, cut into triangles	50 g	2 oz	1/2 cup
Tinned pineapple ring, cut into 8 chunks	1	1	1
Pinch of red food colouring powder			
Sweet and Sour Sauce (page 18) 1 recipe			

1. Thinly slice the beef and place in a bowl with the whisky, sugar and soy sauce. Mix well and leave for about 30 minutes.

2. Heat the oil in a pan, add the marinated beef and stir-fry for 4 minutes. Add the garlic and ginger and stir-fry for 30 seconds. Add the onion, carrot and green pepper and stir-fry for 2 minutes. Add the pineapple and fry for 1 minute.

3. Add the food colouring and sauce and heat through until thickened slightly.

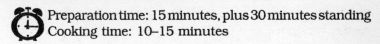 Preparation time: 15 minutes, plus 30 minutes standing
Cooking time: 10–15 minutes

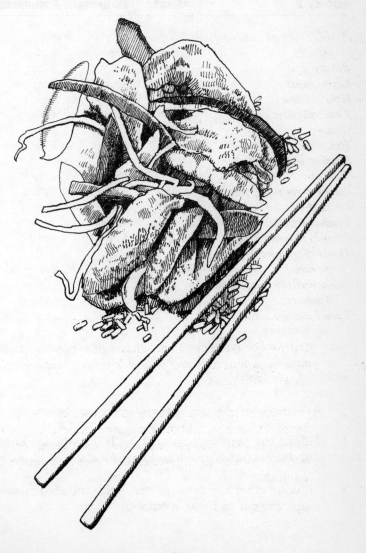

SWEET AND SOUR PRAWNS

This recipe uses a lighter, fluffier batter which you may prefer.

Serves 2	Metric	Imperial	American
Prawns (shrimp), thawed if frozen	225 g	8 oz	2 cups
Whisky	30 ml	2 tbsp	2 tbsp
Brown sugar	10 ml	2 tsp	2 tsp
Light soy sauce	10 ml	2 tsp	2 tsp
Plain (all-purpose) flour	60 ml	4 tbsp	4 tbsp
Water	60 ml	4 tbsp	4 tbsp
Salt	5 ml	1 tsp	1 tsp
Pinch of mustard powder			
Vinegar	5 ml	1 tsp	1 tsp
Oil for deep-frying, plus	30 ml	2 tbsp	2 tbsp
Crushed garlic	2.5 ml	1/2 tsp	1/2 tsp
Crushed fresh root ginger	2.5 ml	1/2 tsp	1/2 tsp
Roughly chopped onion	25 g	1 oz	1 tbsp
Thinly sliced carrot, blanched	15 g	1/2 oz	2 tsp
Green (bell) pepper, cut into triangles	50 g	2 oz	1/2 cup
Tinned pineapple ring, cut into 8 chunks	1	1	1
Pinch of red food colouring powder			
Sweet and Sour Sauce (page 18) 1 recipe			

1. Place the prawns in a bowl with the whisky, sugar and soy sauce. Mix well and leave for about 30 minutes.

2. Mix together the flour, water, salt, mustard powder and vinegar to make a smooth batter.

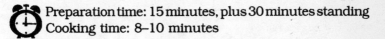

3. Heat the oil for deep-frying.

4. Dip the prawns into the batter, coat thoroughly, then transfer immediately to the oil. Cook for about 3 minutes over a medium heat until golden and cooked through. Remove and drain.

5. Heat the 30 ml/2 tbsp of oil in a pan, and add the garlic and ginger and stir-fry for 30 seconds. Add the onion, carrot and green pepper and stir-fry for 2 minutes. Add the pineapple and fry for 1 minute.

6. Add the food colouring and sauce and heat through until thickened slightly.

Preparation time: 15 minutes, plus 30 minutes standing
Cooking time: 8–10 minutes

CANTONESE-STYLE CHICKEN FILLET

Serves 2	Metric	Imperial	American
Small chicken breasts	2 x 100 g	2 x 4 oz	2 x 4 oz
Light soy sauce	10 ml	2 tsp	2 tsp
Plain (all-purpose) flour	60 ml	4 tbsp	4 tbsp
Water	60 ml	4 tbsp	4 tbsp
Salt	5 ml	1 tsp	1 tsp
Pinch of mustard powder			
Vinegar	5 ml	1 tsp	1 tsp
Oil for deep frying			
Sweet and Sour Sauce (page 18) 1 recipe			

1. Place each chicken breast between clingfilm (plastic wrap) and beat with a rolling pin to flatten slightly.

2. Mix together the flour, water, salt, mustard powder and vinegar to make a smooth batter.

3. Heat the oil for deep-frying.

4. Dip the breasts in the batter and deep-fry for about 5-6 minutes until cooked and deep golden brown. Serve whole, or sliced on a bed of shredded lettuce. Heat the sauce, if using, and pour over the chicken.

Preparation time: 10 minutes
Cooking time: 8 minutes

Cantonese-style Pork Fillet

Follow the recipe for Cantonese-style Chicken Fillet but
substitute 225 g/8 oz/2 cups of thickly sliced pork fillet for
the chicken.

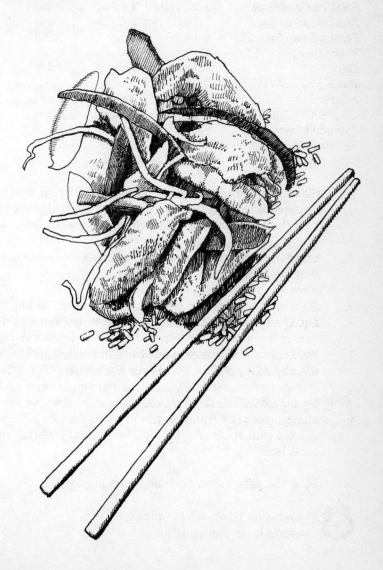

CANTONESE-STYLE FILLET STEAK

Serves 2	Metric	Imperial	American
Fresh root ginger, peeled	50 g	2 oz	1/2 cup
Salt, for sprinkling			
Tomato Sauce (page 22) 1 recipe			
Oil	15 ml	1 tbsp	1 tbsp
Butter	15 ml	1 tbsp	1 tbsp
Fillet steak	2 x 100 g pieces	2 x 4 oz pieces	2 x 4 oz pieces
Tinned pineapple rings	2	2	2
Red glacé (candied) cherries	2	2	2

1. Halve the ginger and slice it along the grain as thinly as possible. Spread it on a plate and sprinkle lightly with the salt. Leave to stand while you heat the sauce.

2. Bring the Tomato Sauce to the boil in a saucepan, then switch off the heat.

3. Squeeze the ginger in your hand to remove as much liquid as possible, then add it to the sauce in the pan.

4. Heat the oil and butter in a frying pan (skillet) and cook the steaks on both sides to your preference. When the steaks are almost ready, add the pineapple rings and fry for about 30 seconds on each side. Remove the steaks from the frying pan and place on two plates. Place a pineapple ring on top of each and a cherry in each hole.

5. Pour the sauce over the steaks and serve.

 Preparation time: 10–12 minutes
Cooking time: About 10 minutes

CANTONESE-STYLE KING PRAWN

Serves 2	Metric	Imperial	American
Egg white	1	1	1
Cornflour (cornstarch)	15 ml	1 tbsp	1 tbsp
Sherry	10 ml	2 tsp	2 tsp
Pinch of salt			
King prawns (jumbo shrimp)	225 g	8 oz	2 cups
Oil	45 ml	3 tbsp	3 tbsp
Crushed garlic	5 ml	1 tsp	1 tsp
Crushed fresh root ginger	5 ml	1 tsp	1 tsp
Spring onions (scallions), chopped	2	2	2
Light soy sauce	15 ml	1 tbsp	1 tbsp
Orange juice	15 ml	1 tbsp	1 tbsp
Sugar	5 ml	1 tsp	1 tsp

1. Mix together thoroughly the egg white, cornflour, sherry and salt to make a batter.

2. Toss the prawns in the batter to coat well.

3. Heat the oil, add the garlic and ginger and stir-fry for 30 seconds.

4. Remove excess batter from the prawns, add to the pan and stir-fry for 3 minutes.

5. Finally, add the spring onion, soy sauce, orange juice and sugar and stir well, coating the prawns.

Preparation time: 10 minutes
Cooking time: 5 minutes

CHICKEN WITH PINEAPPLE

Serves 2	Metric	Imperial	American
Cornflour (cornstarch)	5 ml	1 tsp	1 tsp
Chicken breast, sliced	225 g	8 oz	2 cups
Oil	30 ml	2 tbsp	2 tbsp
Tinned pineapple rings, each cut into 8 chunks	4	4	4
Small green (bell) pepper, cut into triangles	½	½	½
Sugar	10 ml	2 tsp	2 tsp
Sweet and Sour Sauce (page 18) 1 recipe			

1. Mix the cornflour with 5 ml/1 tsp of cold water and marinate the chicken in this mixture for about 15 minutes.

2. Heat the oil and fry (sauté) the chicken for about 3 minutes until just tender and cooked through.

3. Add the pineapple chunks, green pepper and sugar and stir-fry for 2 minutes to heat through.

4. Add the sauce and stir until thickened.

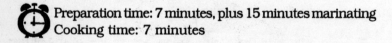 Preparation time: 7 minutes, plus 15 minutes marinating
Cooking time: 7 minutes

Beef with Pineapple

Follow the recipe for Chicken with Pineapple but substitute 225 g/8 oz/2 cups of sliced beef for the chicken.

Pork with Pineapple

Follow the recipe for Chicken with Pineapple but substitute 225 g/8 oz/2 cups of sliced pork for the chicken.

Prawns with Pineapple

Follow the recipe for Chicken with Pineapple but substitute 225 g/8 oz/2 cups of prawns (shrimp) for the chicken.

CHICKEN WITH VEGETABLES

Serves 2	Metric	Imperial	American
Cornflour (cornstarch)	*5 ml*	*1 tsp*	*1 tsp*
Chicken breast, thinly sliced	*225 g*	*8 oz*	*2 cups*
Oil	*30 ml*	*2 tbsp*	*2 tbsp*
Crushed garlic	*5 ml*	*1 tsp*	*1 tsp*
Finely chopped fresh root ginger	*5 ml*	*1 tsp*	*1 tsp*
Button mushrooms, sliced	*50 g*	*2 oz*	*1 cup*
Sliced carrots, blanched	*50 g*	*2 oz*	*¹/₂ cup*
Tinned baby sweetcorn (baby corn)	*4*	*4*	*4*
Peas, thawed	*15 ml*	*1 tbsp*	*1 tbsp*
Chinese leaves or lettuce, shredded	*50 g*	*2 oz*	*4 tbsp*
Light Sauce (page 19) 1 recipe			

1. Mix the cornflour with 5 ml/1 tsp of cold water and marinate the chicken in this mixture for 5 minutes.

2. Heat the oil and stir-fry the garlic and ginger for 30 seconds. Add the chicken and stir-fry until just cooked through.

3. Add the mushrooms, carrots, baby sweetcorn and peas and stir-fry for 1 minute. Add the Chinese leaves or lettuce and stir-fry for 1 minute.

4. Finally, add the sauce and stir-fry until thickened slightly.

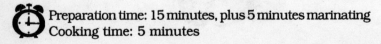 Preparation time: 15 minutes, plus 5 minutes marinating
Cooking time: 5 minutes

Beef with Vegetables

Follow the recipe for Chicken with Vegetables but substitute 225 g/8 oz/2 cups of raw thinly sliced beef for the chicken and 25 g/1 oz/ 2 tbsp of mangetout (snow peas) for the Chinese leaves or lettuce.

Pork with Vegetables

Follow the recipe for Chicken with Vegetables but substitute 225 g/8 oz/2 cups of raw thinly sliced pork for the chicken.

Prawns with Vegetables

Follow the recipe for Chicken with Vegetables but substitute 225 g/8 oz/2 cups of prawns (shrimp) for the chicken, and omit the carrot.

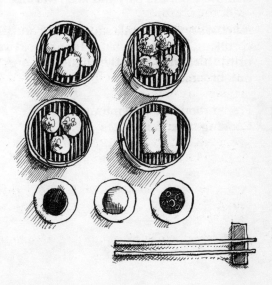

STUFFED CHINESE MUSHROOMS

Serves 2	Metric	Imperial	American
Prawns (shrimp), minced	50 g	2 oz	1/2 cup
Chicken breast, minced	50 g	2 oz	1/2 cup
Cornflour (cornstarch)	10 ml	2 tsp	2 tsp
Dried Chinese mushrooms, reconstituted	8	8	8
Oil	30 ml	2 tbsp	2 tbsp
Light soy sauce	15 ml	1 tbsp	1 tbsp
Sweet chilli sauce	15 ml	1 tbsp	1 tbsp
Sugar	10 ml	2 tsp	2 tsp

1. Mix together the prawns and chicken and 5 ml/1 tsp of the cornflour. Use to stuff the mushrooms.

2. Heat the oil and carefully fry (sauté) the stuffed mushrooms on both sides for about 3 minutes altogether. Remove from the pan and keep warm.

3. Add the soy sauce, chilli sauce, sugar and the remaining cornflour, mixed with 5 ml/1 tsp of cold water. Stir-fry until thickened slightly, then pour over the stuffed mushrooms.

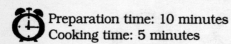 Preparation time: 10 minutes
Cooking time: 5 minutes

Rice &
Noodles

Rice and noodles are the standard accompaniment to many meals. In Chinese cuisine, however, they can be cooked with a delicious range of added ingredients to make them a tasty dish in their own right.

PLAIN BOILED RICE

The two most common ways of serving rice in Chinese take-aways and restaurants are plain boiled or fried. Fried rice has to be boiled first.

The recipe below gives enough rice for two servings. I always boil enough rice for three or four meals and freeze what I don't want to use immediately.

Serves 2	Metric	Imperial	American
Chinese long-grain rice or any other long-grain rice	*150 g*	*5 oz*	*²/₃ cup*
Salt	*5 ml*	*1 tsp*	*1 tsp*

1. Place the rice in a saucepan and pour in plenty of water. With one hand agitate the rice until the water turns cloudy, then discard as much water as possible. Repeat this process two or three times until the water no longer goes cloudy. Drain the rice thoroughly through a sieve and return to the saucepan.

2. Pour in enough water to cover the rice plus about 1 cm/½ in. Add the salt and allow to stand for about 40 minutes.

3. Bring to the boil and continue boiling until the liquid evaporates completely. Stir the rice a couple of times to distribute it in the pan. Switch off the heat, cover the pan and leave for about 5–10 minutes to fluff up.

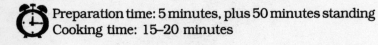 Preparation time: 5 minutes, plus 50 minutes standing
Cooking time: 15–20 minutes

Coloured Rice

Place a pinch of food colouring powder in a cup and add 15 ml/1 tbsp of cold water. Follow the recipe for Plain Boiled Rice and at the point when you switch off the heat dribble the colouring and water mixture all over the surface of the rice. Do not stir at this stage.

Cover the pan and leave for about 5–10 minutes. Stir the rice with a fork and you will find that the colour has spread through the rice to give a speckled effect.

PLAIN FRIED RICE

Serves 2	Metric	Imperial	American
Oil	*15 ml*	*1 tbsp*	*1 tbsp*
Small onion, finely chopped	*1*	*1*	*1*
Salt	*5 ml*	*1 tsp*	*1 tsp*
Pinch of curry powder			
Sesame oil	*5 ml*	*1 tsp*	*1 tsp*
Plain Boiled Rice (page 72)			
* 1 recipe*			

1. Heat the oil in a frying pan (skillet). Add the onion and stir-fry over medium heat for about 5 minutes until soft and lightly golden.

2. Reduce the heat to low. Add the salt, curry powder, sesame oil and the plain boiled rice. Stir-fry and mix until all the ingredients are thoroughly combined and the rice is hot.

 Preparation time: 2 minutes
Cooking time: 10 minutes

EGG FRIED RICE

Serves 2	Metric	Imperial	American
Oil	30 ml	2 tbsp	2 tbsp
Egg, beaten	1	1	1
Onion, thinly sliced	½	½	½
Lean bacon rashers (slices), chopped	2	2	2
Peas, thawed	30 ml	2 tbsp	2 tbsp
Salt	5 ml	1 tsp	1 tsp
Plain Boiled Rice (page 72) 1 recipe			

1. Heat 15 ml/1 tbsp of the oil in a pan and add the egg. Stir with a wooden spoon or fork until it is cooked and scrambled into small pieces. Remove to a plate and set aside.

2. Heat the remaining oil in a frying pan (skillet) and stir-fry the onion for about 3 minutes until pale but golden.

3. Add the bacon and stir-fry for about 3 minutes until cooked.

4. Add the peas, salt and rice and stir thoroughly to heat through. Finally, add the egg and stir through gently for about 2 minutes.

Preparation time: 5 minutes
Cooking time: 10 minutes

CHICKEN FRIED RICE

Serves 2	Metric	Imperial	American
Oil	*30 ml*	*2 tbsp*	*2 tbsp*
Egg, beaten	*1*	*1*	*1*
Precooked Chicken (page 23), roughly shredded	*100 g*	*4 oz*	*1 cup*
Plain Boiled Rice (page 72) 1 recipe			
Peas, thawed	*30 ml*	*2 tbsp*	*2 tbsp*
Salt	*5 ml*	*1 tsp*	*1 tsp*
Light soy sauce	*15 ml*	*1 tbsp*	*1 tbsp*

1. Heat 15 ml/1 tbsp of the oil in a pan and add the egg. Stir with a wooden spoon or fork until it is cooked and scrambled into small pieces. Remove to a plate and set aside.

2. Heat the remaining oil in a frying pan (skillet) and add the chicken. Stir-fry for 2 minutes.

3. Add the rice, peas, salt and soy sauce and stir-fry for about 3 minutes until heated through.

 Preparation time: 5 minutes
Cooking time: 6 minutes

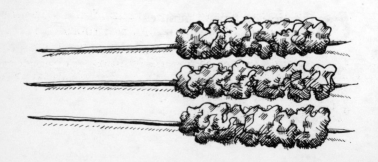

BEEF FRIED RICE

Serves 2	Metric	Imperial	American
Oil	30 ml	2 tbsp	2 tbsp
Egg, beaten	1	1	1
Garlic clove, crushed	1	1	1
Crushed fresh root ginger	5 ml	1 tsp	1 tsp
Precooked Mince (page 24)	100 g	4 oz	1 cup
Plain Boiled Rice (page 72) 1 recipe			
Sugar	5 ml	1 tsp	1 tsp
Salt	5 ml	1 tsp	1 tsp
Dark soy sauce	5 ml	1 tsp	1 tsp
Small pinch of five spice powder			
Chopped fresh coriander (cilantro)	15 ml	1 tbsp	1 tbsp
Spring onion (scallion), finely chopped	1	1	1

1. Heat 15 ml/1 tbsp of the oil in a pan and add the egg. Stir with a wooden spoon or fork until it is cooked and scrambled into small pieces. Remove to a plate and set aside.

2. Heat the remaining oil, add the garlic, ginger and the mince and stir-fry for 2 minutes.

3. Add the rice, sugar, salt, soy sauce, five spice powder, coriander and spring onion. Stir thoroughly until heated through, then add the cooked egg. Stir through gently for about 2 minutes.

Preparation time: 5 minutes
Cooking time: 5 minutes

PRAWN FRIED RICE

Serves 2	Metric	Imperial	American
Oil	30 ml	2 tbsp	2 tbsp
Egg, beaten	1	1	1
Prawns (shrimp)	175 g	6 oz	1½ cups
Bean sprouts	25 g	1 oz	1 oz
Spring onion (scallion), finely chopped	1	1	1
Peas, thawed	30 ml	2 tbsp	2 tbsp
Dried Chinese mushrooms, reconstituted and thinly sliced	2	2	2
Light soy sauce	10 ml	2 tsp	2 tsp
Salt	5 ml	1 tsp	1 tsp
Plain Boiled Rice (page 72) 1 recipe			

1. Heat 15 ml/1 tbsp of the oil in a pan and add the egg. Stir with a wooden spoon or fork until it is cooked and scrambled into small pieces. Remove to a plate and set aside.

2. Heat the remaining oil and stir-fry the prawns, bean sprouts, spring onion, peas, Chinese mushrooms, soy sauce and salt for 2 minutes.

3. Add the boiled rice and stir into the ingredients in the pan until evenly distributed and heated through.

Preparation time: 2 minutes
Cooking time: 5 minutes

SPECIAL FRIED RICE

Serves 2	Metric	Imperial	American
Oil	15 ml	1 tbsp	1 tbsp
Small onion, thinly sliced	½	½	½
Chinese curry powder	10 ml	2 tsp	2 tsp
Prawns (shrimp)	50 g	2 oz	2 oz
Precooked Chicken (page 23), roughly shredded	50 g	2 oz	2 oz
Precooked Mince (page 24)	50 g	2 oz	2 oz
Dried Chinese mushrooms, reconstituted and thinly sliced	2	2	2
Plain Boiled Rice (page 72) 1 recipe			
Salt	5 ml	1 tsp	1 tsp
Peas, thawed	30 ml	2 tbsp	2 tbsp

1. Heat the oil and add the onion. Stir-fry for 5 minutes until golden.

2. Mix the curry powder to a paste with 10 ml/2 tsp of cold water and add to the onion with the prawns, chicken, mince and mushrooms. Stir-fry for 3 minutes.

3. Add the rice, salt and peas and stir gently until heated through.

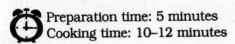
Preparation time: 5 minutes
Cooking time: 10–12 minutes

FRIED NOODLES

Serves 2	Metric	Imperial	American
Egg noodles	175 g	6 oz	1½ cups
Oil	30 ml	2 tbsp	2 tbsp
Crushed fresh root ginger	15 ml	1 tbsp	1 tbsp
Crushed garlic	10 ml	2 tsp	2 tsp
Sugar	5 ml	1 tsp	1 tsp
Dark soy sauce	15 ml	1 tbsp	1 tbsp
Light soy sauce	15 ml	1 tbsp	1 tbsp

1. Cook the noodles in a pan of boiling water for about 6 minutes until soft, or follow the instructions on the packet. Drain and rinse in cold water, then leave aside to drain again.

2. Heat the oil and fry (sauté) the ginger and garlic for 1 minute without browning.

3. Add the noodles and stir-fry for about 2 minutes. Add the sugar and soy sauces and stir-fry until the noodles are coated with sauce.

 Preparation time: 2 minutes
Cooking time: 10 minutes

SESAME FRIED NOODLES

Serves 2	Metric	Imperial	American
Chinese egg noodles	*175 g*	*6 oz*	*1½ cups*
Sesame oil	*15 ml*	*1 tbsp*	*1 tbsp*
Finely chopped fresh root			
ginger	*10 ml*	*2 tsp*	*2 tsp*
Sesame seeds	*10 ml*	*2 tsp*	*2 tsp*
Light soy sauce	*5 ml*	*1 tsp*	*1 tsp*
Sweet chilli sauce	*5 ml*	*1 tsp*	*1 tsp*

1. Cook the noodles in boiling water for about 6 minutes, or follow the instructions on the packet. Drain well and dry.

2. Heat the oil and stir-fry the ginger for 30 seconds. Add all the remaining ingredients, including the noodles. Stir-fry until the noodles are thoroughly coated with the sauce.

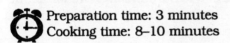 Preparation time: 3 minutes
Cooking time: 8–10 minutes

81

CHICKEN CHOW MEIN

Serves 2	Metric	Imperial	American
Cornflour (cornstarch)	10 ml	2 tsp	2 tsp
Chicken breast, sliced	225 g	8 oz	2 cups
Medium egg noodles	225 g	8 oz	2 cups
Oil	45 ml	3 tbsp	3 tbsp
Dried Chinese mushrooms, reconstituted and sliced	2	2	2
Button mushrooms, sliced	50 g	2 oz	1 cup
Tinned bamboo shoots, sliced	50 g	2 oz	1 cup
Crushed fresh root ginger	5 ml	1 tsp	1 tsp
Crushed garlic	5 ml	1 tsp	1 tsp
Sesame oil	5 ml	1 tsp	1 tsp
Chilli Sauce (page 20) 1 recipe			

1. Mix the cornflour with 10 ml/2 tsp of cold water and marinate the chicken in this mixture for about 15 minutes.

2. Cook the noodles in a pan of boiling water for about 6 minutes until soft, or follow the instructions on the packet. Drain and rinse in cold water. Leave aside to drain again.

3. Heat the oil in a frying pan (skillet) and stir-fry the chicken for 3 minutes.

4. Add the Chinese mushrooms, button mushrooms, bamboo shoots, ginger and garlic and stir-fry for 3 minutes.

5. Add the drained noodles and stir-fry for 2 minutes.

6. Add the sesame oil and sauce and cook until thickened and the sauce coats the noodles.

Preparation time: 10 minutes, plus 15 minutes marinating
Cooking time: 15–18 minutes

Beef Chow Mein

Follow the Recipe for Chicken Chow Mein but substitute 225 g/8 oz/2 cups of sliced beef for the chicken and cook for 5 minutes. Add 100 g/4 oz/1 cup of peeled sliced cucumber at step 4.

Pork Chow Mein

Follow the recipe for Chicken Chow Mein but substitute 225 g/8 oz/2 cups of sliced pork for the chicken.

Prawn Chow Mein

Follow the recipe for Chicken Chow Mein but substitute 225 g/8 oz/2 cups of prawns (shrimp) for the chicken and cook for 1 minute only.

Special Chow Mein

Follow the recipe for Chicken Chow Mein but reduce the amount of chicken to 100 g/4 oz/1 cup and add 100 g/4 oz/1 cup of sliced beef to the marinade at step 1. Add 50 g/2 oz/¹/₂ cup of thawed prawns with the noodles at step 5.

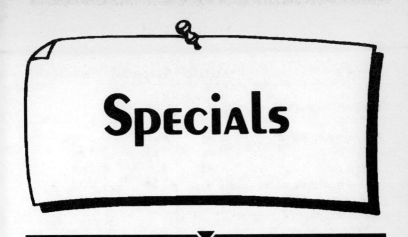

Specials

Here is a selection of dishes to add to any special occasion. They are no more difficult to prepare than the main dishes already given, but they have that certain 'something' that makes them that little bit more impressive.

SHREDDED SPICY CHICKEN

Serves 2	Metric	Imperial	American
Cornflour (cornstarch)	5 ml	1 tsp	1 tsp
Egg white	1	1	1
Chicken breast, sliced	225 g	8 oz	2 cups
Oil	45 ml	3 tbsp	3 tbsp
Crushed garlic	10 ml	2 tsp	2 tsp
Crushed fresh root ginger	10 ml	2 tsp	2 tsp
Sliced green (bell) pepper	100 g	4 oz	4 oz
Dark Sauce (page 17) 1 recipe			
Five spice powder	2.5 ml	½ tsp	½ tsp
Finely chopped spring onion (scallion)	15 ml	1 tbsp	1 tbsp

1. Mix together the cornflour and the egg white and marinate the chicken in this mixture for about 10 minutes.

2. Heat the oil, lift the chicken out of the marinade and stir-fry for about 3 minutes.

3. Add the garlic, ginger and green pepper and stir-fry for 2 minutes.

4. Finally, add the sauce and five spice powder and cook until thickened slightly. Sprinkle on the spring onion.

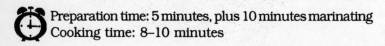 Preparation time: 5 minutes, plus 10 minutes marinating
Cooking time: 8–10 minutes

Shredded Spicy Beef

Follow the recipe for Shredded Spicy Chicken but substitute 225 g/8 oz/2 cups of raw sliced beef for the chicken, and add 100 g/4 oz/1 cup of cashew nuts at step 3.

Shredded Spicy Prawns

Follow the recipe for Shredded Spicy Chicken but substitute 225 g/8 oz/2 cups of raw prawns (shrimp) for the chicken.

CHICKEN IN FRAGRANT LEMON SAUCE

Serves 2	Metric	Imperial	American
For the batter			
Whisky	30 ml	2 tbsp	2 tbsp
Brown sugar	10 ml	2 tsp	2 tsp
Light soy sauce	10 ml	2 tsp	2 tsp
Cornflour (cornstarch)	90 ml	6 tbsp	6 tbsp
or			
Plain (all-purpose) flour	60 ml	4 tbsp	4 tbsp
Water	60 ml	4 tbsp	4 tbsp
Salt	5 ml	1 tsp	1 tsp
Pinch of mustard powder			
Vinegar	5 ml	1 tsp	1 tsp
Chicken breast, sliced	225 g	8 oz	2 cups
Oil for deep frying			
For the lemon sauce			
Sugar	45 ml	3 tbsp	3 tbsp
Lemon juice	45 ml	3 tbsp	3 tbsp
Lemon zest	5 ml	1 tsp	1 tsp
Cornflour	5 ml	1 tsp	1 tsp
Oil	10 ml	2 tsp	2tsp

1. Place the whisky, sugar, soy sauce and 10 ml/2 tsp of cornflour in a bowl with the chicken. Mix well and leave for about 30 minutes.

2. Add 15-20 ml/3-4 tsp of cornflour to give a thickish batter which just coats the chicken.

3.   Place the remaining cornflour on a plate and, with one hand, lift pieces of chicken with as much batter as possible and quickly transfer to the plate. Roll in the dry cornflour, then remove and place on a clean plate. Repeat until all the chicken has been used up. Allow to sit for about 5 minutes before frying.

4.   Alternatively mix together the flour, water, salt, mustard powder and vinegar to make a smooth batter. Dip the chicken in the batter and immediately transfer to the hot oil for frying.

5.   Whichever batter has been used, heat the oil for deep-frying and add the battered chicken. Cook for about 4 minutes over medium heat until golden and cooked through. Remove and drain.

6.   Mix together all the sauce ingredients except the oil.

7.   Heat the oil in a pan and add the sauce. Cook until thickened slightly, and pour over the chicken.

Preparation time: 15 minutes, plus 35 minutes standing, or 5 minutes
Cooking time: 8–10 minutes

Pork in Fragrant Lemon Sauce

Follow the recipe for Chicken in Fragrant Lemon Sauce but substitute 225 g/8 oz/2 cups of raw sliced pork for the chicken.

Prawns in Fragrant Lemon Sauce

Follow the recipe for Chicken in Fragrant Lemon Sauce but substitute 225 g/8 oz/2 cups of prawns (shrimp) for the chicken.

BEEF IN FRAGRANT LEMON SAUCE

Serves 2	Metric	Imperial	American
Oil	15 ml	1 tbsp	1 tbsp
Crushed fresh root ginger	5 ml	1 tsp	1 tsp
Beef, sliced	225 g	8 oz	2 cups
For the lemon sauce			
Sugar	45 ml	3 tbsp	3 tbsp
Lemon juice	45 ml	3 tbsp	3 tbsp
Lemon zest	5 ml	1 tsp	1 tsp
Cornflour	5 ml	1 tsp	1 tsp

1. Heat the oil and stir-fry the ginger for about 30 seconds.

2. Add the beef and stir-fry for about 5 minutes, or until cooked.

3. Put the sauce ingredients in a saucepan and heat gently until thickened slightly. Pour over the beef.

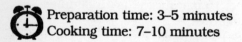 Preparation time: 3–5 minutes
Cooking time: 7–10 minutes

SKEWERED CHICKEN

Serves 2	Metric	Imperial	American
Chicken breast, cut into 2.5 cm (1 in) cubes	225 g	8 oz	2 cups
For the marinade			
Chinese curry powder	15 ml	1 tbsp	1 tbsp
Oil	15 ml	1 tbsp	1 tbsp
Pinch of salt			
Finely chopped coriander (cilantro)	10 ml	2 tsp	2 tsp

1. Mix together all the marinade ingredients in a glass bowl. Add the chicken and coat well, using your hands. Cover and marinate for up to 24 hours in the fridge.

2. When ready to cook, preheat the grill (broiler). Take the chicken cubes and thread them on to metal skewers. Place on a foil-lined baking tray and grill (broil) for about 5 minutes on each side.

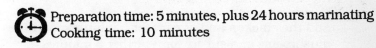

Preparation time: 5 minutes, plus 24 hours marinating
Cooking time: 10 minutes

SLICED CHICKEN WITH OYSTER SAUCE

Serves 2	Metric	Imperial	American
Cornflour (cornstarch)	10 ml	2 tsp	2 tsp
Chicken breast, thinly sliced	225 g	8 oz	2 cups
Oil	30 ml	2 tbsp	2 tbsp
Crushed garlic	5 ml	1 tsp	1 tsp
Crushed fresh root ginger	5 ml	1 tsp	1 tsp
Button mushrooms, sliced	50 g	2 oz	1 cup
Oyster sauce	45 ml	3 tbsp	3 tbsp
Light soy sauce	15 ml	1 tbsp	1 tbsp
Sugar	10 ml	2 tsp	2 tsp

1. Mix 5 ml/1 tsp of the cornflour with 5 ml/1 tsp of cold water and marinate the chicken in this mixture for about 15 minutes.

2. Heat the oil and stir-fry the garlic and ginger for 30 seconds.

3. Add the chicken and stir-fry for 3 minutes. Add the mushrooms and stir-fry for a further 3 minutes.

4. Finally, add the oyster sauce, soy sauce, sugar and the remaining 5 ml/1 tsp of cornflour mixed with 5 ml/1 tsp of cold water. Cook until thickened slightly.

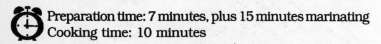
Preparation time: 7 minutes, plus 15 minutes marinating
Cooking time: 10 minutes

Sliced Beef with Oyster Sauce

Follow the recipe for Sliced Chicken with Oyster Sauce but substitute 225 g/8 oz/2 cups of thinly sliced raw beef for the chicken.

Sliced Pork with Oyster Sauce

Follow the recipe for Sliced Chicken with Oyster Sauce but substitute 225 g/8 oz/2 cups of thinly sliced raw pork for the chicken.

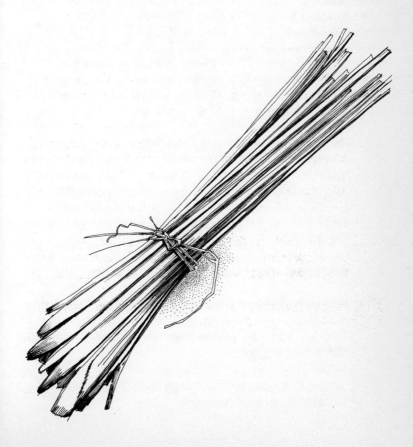

CHICKEN AND PINEAPPLE WITH CELERY

Serves 2	Metric	Imperial	American
Cornflour (cornstarch)	5 ml	1 tsp	1 tsp
Chicken breast, thinly sliced	225 g	8 oz	2 cups
Oil	30 ml	2 tbsp	2 tbsp
Crushed garlic	10 ml	2 tsp	2 tsp
Crushed fresh root ginger	10 ml	2 tsp	2 tsp
Celery stick, thinly sliced	1	1	1
Tinned pineapple rings, each cut into 8 chunks	2	2	2
For the lemon and pineapple sauce			
Sugar	45 ml	3 tbsp	3 tbsp
Lemon juice	45 ml	3 tbsp	3 tbsp
Pineapple juice	45 ml	3 tbsp	3 tbsp
Cornflour (cornstarch)	10 ml	2 tsp	2 tsp

1. Mix the 5 ml/1 tsp of cornflour with 5 ml/1 tsp of cold water and marinate the chicken in this mixture for 15 minutes.

2. Heat the oil and stir-fry the garlic and ginger for 30 seconds.

3. Add the chicken and stir-fry for 3 minutes.

4. Add the celery and pineapple and stir-fry for 2 minutes.

5. Finally, add the sauce ingredients and cook until thickened slightly.

 Preparation time: 10 minutes, plus 15 minutes marinating
Cooking time: 6–10 minutes

Beef and Pineapple with Celery

Follow the recipe for Chicken and Pineapple with Celery but substitute 225 g/8 oz/2 cups of raw sliced beef for the chicken, and add 100 g/4 oz/1 cup of salted peanuts or cashew nuts at step 4.

Pork and Pineapple with Celery

Follow the recipe for Chicken and Pineapple with Celery but substitute 225 g/8 oz/2 cups of raw sliced pork for the chicken.

Prawn and Pineapple with Celery

Follow the recipe for Chicken and Pineapple with Celery but substitute 225 g/8 oz/2 cups of prawns (shrimp) for the chicken, and add 30 ml/2 tbsp of finely chopped spring onion (scallion) at step 4.

CHICKEN WITH GINGER AND BAMBOO SHOOTS

Serves 2	Metric	Imperial	American
Cornflour (cornstarch)	5 ml	1 tsp	1 tsp
Chicken breast, thinly sliced	225 g	8 oz	2 cups
Oil	30 ml	2 tbsp	2 tbsp
Finely chopped fresh root ginger	15 ml	1 tbsp	1 tbsp
Crushed garlic	10 ml	2 tsp	2 tsp
Green (bell) pepper, cut into triangles	100 g	4 oz	1 cup
Roughly chopped onion	50 g	2 oz	¹/₂ cup
Bamboo shoots, sliced	50 g	2 oz	¹/₂ cup
Tomato Sauce (page 22) 1 recipe			

1. Mix the cornflour with 5 ml/1 tsp of cold water and marinate the chicken in this mixture for about 15 minutes.

2. Heat the oil and stir-fry the ginger and garlic for 1 minute without browning.

3. Add the chicken and stir-fry for 3 minutes.

4. Add the green pepper, onion and bamboo shoots and stir-fry for 2 minutes.

5. Finally, add the sauce and cook until slightly thickened.

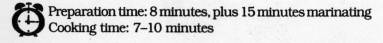 Preparation time: 8 minutes, plus 15 minutes marinating
Cooking time: 7–10 minutes

Beef with Ginger and Bamboo Shoots

Follow the recipe for Chicken with Ginger and Bamboo Shoots but substitute 225 g/8 oz/2 cups of raw sliced beef for the chicken.

Pork with Ginger and Bamboo Shoots

Follow the recipe for Chicken with Ginger and Bamboo Shoots but substitute 225 g/8 oz/2 cups of raw sliced pork for the chicken.

Prawns with Ginger and Bamboo Shoots

Follow the recipe for Chicken with Ginger and Bamboo Shoots but substitute 225 g/8 oz/2 cups of prawns (shrimp) for the chicken, and add 15 ml/1 tbsp of finely chopped coriander (cilantro) leaves at step 5.

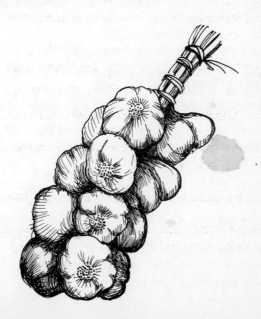

CHAR SHIU

Serves 2–4	Metric	Imperial	American
Whole pork fillet about	450-900 g	1-2 lb	1-2 lb
For the marinade			
Sugar	45 ml	3 tbsp	3 tbsp
Sherry	15 ml	1 tbsp	1 tbsp
Hoisin sauce	15 ml	1 tbsp	1 tbsp
Yellow bean sauce	15 ml	1 tbsp	1 tbsp
Light soy sauce	30 ml	2 tbsp	2 tbsp
Dark soy sauce	15 ml	1 tbsp	1 tbsp
Pinch of red food colouring powder			
Crushed garlic	5 ml	1 tsp	1 tsp
Pinch of five spice powder			
Sweet chilli sauce	15 ml	1 tbsp	1 tbsp
Sesame oil	10 ml	2 tsp	2 tsp
Red wine vinegar	5 ml	1 tsp	1 tsp
For the glaze			
Honey	15 ml	1 tbsp	1 tbsp

1. Mix together all the ingredients for the marinade.

2. Take the pork fillet and make about four 5 mm/¼ in deep cuts diagonally on both the top and bottom surfaces of the fillet without cutting right through.

3. Place the pork in the marinade and leave for up to 24 hours, turning from time to time and coating with the marinade.

4. When ready to cook, preheat the oven to 190°C/ 375°F/gas mark 5. Place a wire cooling rack on a baking sheet with a lip (or use a flat casserole dish (Dutch oven)), remove the pork from the marinade and place on the rack. Cook for 30 minutes in the oven. Then baste with the remaining marinade and cook for a further 20 minutes or so.

5. Remove from the oven and spread the glaze over the top and sides. Leave to go cold, then slice diagonally.

 Preparation time: 10 minutes, plus 24 hours marinating
Cooking time: 50 minutes, plus cooling

LEMON CHICKEN

Serves 2	Metric	Imperial	American
Plain (all-purpose) flour	15 ml	1 tbsp	1 tbsp
Salt	2.5 ml	½ tsp	½ tsp
Five spice powder	2.5 ml	½ tsp	½ tsp
Chicken breast, thinly sliced	225 g	8 oz	2 cups
Oil	15 ml	1 tbsp	1 tbsp
Lemon juice	30 ml	2 tbsp	2 tbsp
Sugar	10 ml	2 tsp	2 tsp

1. Mix together the flour, salt and five spice powder and dip the chicken in this mixture.

2. Heat the oil and stir-fry the chicken for 3 minutes.

3. Take 5 ml/1 tsp of the remaining seasoned flour and mix it with the lemon juice and sugar and 50 ml/2 fl oz/3½ tbsp of cold water. Add this sauce to the chicken and cook for 5 minutes until thickened slightly.

 Preparation time: 5–8 minutes
Cooking time: 8–10 minutes

SZECHUAN CHICKEN

Serves 2	Metric	Imperial	American
Oil	*30 ml*	*2 tbsp*	*2 tbsp*
Crushed garlic	*5 ml*	*1 tsp*	*1 tsp*
Crushed fresh root ginger	*5 ml*	*1 tsp*	*1 tsp*
Green (bell) pepper, cut into triangles	*100 g*	*4 oz*	*1 cup*
Precooked Chicken Breast (page 23), sliced	*225 g*	*8 oz*	*2 cups*
For the sauce			
Sugar	*15 ml*	*1 tbsp*	*1 tbsp*
Black bean paste	*10 ml*	*2 tsp*	*2 tsp*
Sesame oil	*5 ml*	*1 tsp*	*1 tsp*
Light soy sauce	*15 ml*	*1 tbsp*	*1 tbsp*
Water	*15 ml*	*1 tbsp*	*1 tbsp*
Cornflour (cornstarch)	*5 ml*	*1 tsp*	*1 tsp*

1. Mix together all the sauce ingredients.

2. Heat the oil and stir-fry the garlic and ginger for 30 seconds. Add the pepper and stir-fry for 2 minutes.

3. Add the chicken and stir-fry for 1 minute. Add the sauce and stir-fry until thickened slightly.

Preparation time: 7 minutes
Cooking time: 6 minutes

Szechuan Beef

Follow the recipe for Szechuan Chicken but substitute 225 g/8 oz/2 cups of sliced Precooked Beef (page 24) for the chicken.

Szechuan Pork

Follow the recipe for Szechuan Chicken but substitute 225 g/8 oz/2 cups of sliced Precooked Pork (page 24) for the chicken.

Szechuan Prawns

Follow the recipe for Szechuan Chicken but substitute 225 g/8 oz/2 cups of raw prawns (shrimp) for the chicken, and cook for 3 minutes instead of 1 minute.

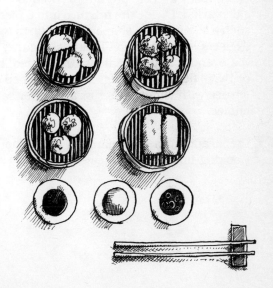

CHINESE BEEFBURGERS

Serves 2	Metric	Imperial	American
Chinese curry powder	*10 ml*	*2 tsp*	*2 tsp*
Pinch of five spice powder			
Minced (ground) beef	*225 g*	*8 oz*	*2 cups*
Finely chopped coriander			
(cilantro)	*15 ml*	*1 tbsp*	*1 tbsp*
Salt	*5 ml*	*1 tsp*	*1 tsp*

1. Mix the curry powder and five spice powder together in a cup with 5 ml/1 tsp of cold water.

2. Mix together all the remaining ingredients and the curry paste. Knead well with your hands, or process for about 15 seconds in a food processor, until smooth. Leave for the flavours to develop for up to 2 hours.

3. When ready to cook, preheat the oven to 190°C/375°F/gas mark 5. Divide the mixture into 6 pieces and form each into a sausage shape. Thread on to two long metal skewers, place on a foil-lined baking tray and cook in the oven for approximately 20 minutes, turning once or twice during cooking. Serve on a bed of shredded lettuce with lemon sauce or any other sauce of your choice.

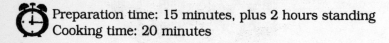 Preparation time: 15 minutes, plus 2 hours standing
Cooking time: 20 minutes

CHINESE RISSOLES

Serves 2	Metric	Imperial	American
Minced (ground) beef	*225 g*	*8 oz*	*2 cups*
Very finely chopped onion	*50 g*	*2 oz*	*¹/₂ cup*
Small potato, finely grated	*1*	*1*	*1*
Chinese curry powder	*20 ml*	*4 tsp*	*4 tsp*
Salt	*5 ml*	*1 tsp*	*1 tsp*
Plain (all-purpose) flour	*25 g*	*1 oz*	*2 tbsp*
Oil for deep-frying			

1. Mix together all the ingredients except the oil and knead well with your hands for about 2 minutes.

2. With wet hands, form the mixture into rissoles about 7.5 cm/3 in across.

3. Deep-fry for about 2 minutes until dark brown. Serve on a bed of shredded lettuce with lemon sauce or any other sauce of your choice.

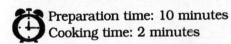

Preparation time: 10 minutes
Cooking time: 2 minutes

SPECIAL CHICKEN SPRING ROLLS

Serves 2	Metric	Imperial	American
Spring roll wrappers (page 16)	*8*	*8*	*8*
For the filling			
Oil	*15 ml*	*1 tbsp*	*1 tbsp*
Chicken breast, minced or very finely chopped	*100 g*	*4 oz*	*1 cup*
Crushed fresh root ginger	*10 ml*	*2 tsp*	*2 tsp*
Crushed garlic	*10 ml*	*2 tsp*	*2 tsp*
Finely chopped spring onion (scallion)	*15 ml*	*1 tbsp*	*1 tbsp*
Dark soy sauce	*5 ml*	*1 tsp*	*1 tsp*
Light soy sauce	*5 ml*	*1 tsp*	*1 tsp*
Sugar	*5 ml*	*1 tsp*	*1 tsp*
Cornflour (cornstarch)	*5 ml*	*1 tsp*	*1 tsp*
For the paste			
Plain (all-purpose) flour	*15 ml*	*1 tbsp*	*1 tbsp*

1. To make the filling, heat the oil and stir-fry the chicken, breaking it up with a spatula if it clumps together.

2. Add the ginger and garlic and stir-fry for 30 seconds.

3. Add the spring onion, soy sauces, sugar and the cornflour mixed with 5 ml/1 tsp of cold water and stir-fry until thickened slightly. Allow to cool.

4. To make the paste, mix the flour with 15 ml/1 tbsp of cold water.

5. To fill the rolls, place about 25 g/1 oz/2 tbsp of the filling in a strip 5 cm/2 in in from each side and the base of the wrapper. Fold the unfilled piece at the base over to cover the filling. Fold the unfilled right side over the filling towards the left and the unfilled left side over the filling towards the right. Now roll up tightly and seal the join of the roll with the flour and water paste. (See diagram on page 33)

6. Deep-fry the prepared spring rolls in oil heated to 180°C/350°F for about 5 minutes until golden brown.

 Preparation time: 15 minutes
Cooking time: 10 minutes

Special Beef Spring Rolls

Follow the recipe for Special Chicken Spring Rolls but substitute 100 g/4 oz/1 cup of Precooked Mince (page 24) for the chicken, and add 2 reconstituted and chopped dried Chinese mushrooms at step 2.

Special Pork Spring Rolls

Follow the recipe for Special Chicken Spring Rolls but substitute 100 g/4 oz/1 cup of minced or finely chopped pork for the chicken.

Special Prawn Spring Rolls

Follow the recipe for Special Chicken Spring Rolls but substitute 100 g/4 oz/1 cup of minced or finely chopped prawns (shrimp) for the chicken, and add 25 g/1 oz/2 tbsp of bean sprouts at step 2.

CHICKEN IN PAPER

Serves 2	Metric	Imperial	American
Rice paper, cut to 13 cm (5 in) square	*8 sheets*	*8 sheets*	*8 sheets*
Chicken breast, halved and thinly sliced	*150 g*	*5 oz*	*1¹/₄ cups*
Oil for deep frying			
For the marinade			
Dark soy sauce	*5 ml*	*1 tsp*	*1 tsp*
Hoisin sauce	*5 ml*	*1 tsp*	*1 tsp*
Sugar	*5 ml*	*1 tsp*	*1 tsp*
Crushed garlic	*5 ml*	*1 tsp*	*1 tsp*
Finely chopped fresh root ginger	*5 ml*	*1 tsp*	*1 tsp*
Sesame oil	*5 ml*	*1 tsp*	*1 tsp*
Pinch of five spice powder			
For the paste			
Plain (all-purpose) flour	*15 ml*	*1 tbsp*	*1 tbsp*

1. Mix together the marinade ingredients in a glass bowl. Add the chicken and coat well. Leave for about 15 minutes.

2. To make the paste, mix the flour with 15 ml/1 tbsp of cold water.

3. Place equal amounts of the mixture in the centre of each square of rice paper, then enclose as in the diagram. Moisten the edges with the flour and water paste to secure.

4. Heat the oil and fry the envelopes for about 4 minutes until golden.

5. Serve with a bottled dipping sauce such as lemon, or Tomato Sauce (page 22), or a sauce made from 45 ml/ 3 tbsp of tomato ketchup (catsup) mixed with 15 ml/ 1 tbsp of dark soy sauce, a pinch of five spice powder, 5 ml/1 tsp of sesame oil and 5 ml/1 tsp of sugar.

Preparation time: 10–15 minutes, plus 15 minutes marinating
Cooking time: 5 minutes

FLOUR AND
WATER PASTE

CHINESE TRIANGLES

In this recipe I use home-made samosa pastry (paste). The recipe for this is in my book *Quick and Easy Indian Meals in Minutes* (Foulsham, 1996) and is reproduced below. However, you can use spring roll wrappers instead.

Serves 2	Metric	Imperial	American
For the filling			
Oil	30 ml	2 tbsp	2 tbsp
Finely chopped onion	175 g	6 oz	1½ cups
Chinese curry powder	15 ml	1 tbsp	1 tbsp
Minced (ground) beef	100 g	4 oz	1 cup
Potatoes, diced and par-boiled until just tender	2 large	2 large	2 large
Peas, thawed	15 ml	1 tbsp	1 tbsp
Finely chopped coriander (cilantro)	15 ml	1 tbsp	1 tbsp
Salt	5 ml	1 tsp	1 tsp
For the pastry (paste)			
Ghee or butter	50 g	2 oz	¼ cup
Strong (bread) flour	225 g	8 oz	2 cups
Salt	5 ml	1 tsp	1 tsp
Hot water	85-120 ml	3-4 fl oz	5½-7 tbsp
Oil for deep frying			

1. To make the filling, heat the oil and stir-fry the onion until golden. Add the curry powder, mixed with 30 ml/ 2 tbsp of cold water, and the beef and stir-fry for 5 minutes.

2. Add the potato, peas, coriander and salt. Mix well together, then leave to go cold.

3.   To make the pastry, rub the fat into the flour until it resembles fine breadcrumbs. Add the salt and mix to a stiffish dough with the hot water. Chill in the fridge for about an hour.

4.   Divide the pastry into eight and roll each piece on a lightly floured surface into as thin a circle as possible. (The thinner the pastry the crisper it will be when fried.)

5.   Heat a frying pan (skillet) until hot, then place each pastry circle in the pan and cook for no more than 10-15 seconds on each side, at the same time pressing down gently with a tea-cloth to make little bubbles rise on the surface. Remove from the pan and cut each circle in half.

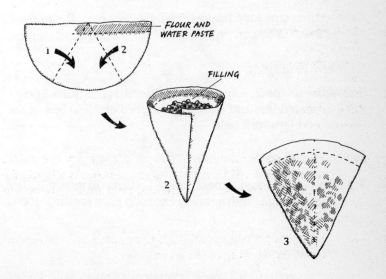

6. Make a thickish paste in a cup with about 10 ml/2 tsp of flour and 5 ml/1 tsp of water. Take one of the half-circles and brush some flour paste along the straight edge. Now form the half-circle into a cone shape and put in about 2 tsp of the cold filling. Brush the top inside edge with the flour paste and press tightly together. Prepare the remaining triangles in the same way.

7. Deep-fry the triangles three at a time for about 4-5 minutes until golden. Make sure the heat is not too high.

Preparation time: 10 minutes, plus cooling; 10 minutes, plus 1 hour chilling
Cooking time: 10–15 minutes

Vegetarian Triangles

Follow the recipe for Chinese Triangles but omit the minced (ground) beef. You can replace it with diced mixed vegetables.

Chicken Triangles

Follow the recipe for Chinese Triangles but substitute 100 g/4 oz of minced (ground) or finely chopped chicken breast for the minced (ground) beef.

Pork Triangles

Follow the recipe for Chinese Triangles but substitute 100 g/4 oz of minced (ground) or finely chopped pork for the minced (ground) beef.

Prawn Triangles

Follow the recipe for Chinese Triangles but substitute 100 g/4 oz of minced (ground) or finely chopped prawns (shrimp) for the minced (ground) beef.

SPECIAL CHINESE CURRY

Serves 2	Metric	Imperial	American
Chinese curry powder	30 ml	2 tbsp	2 tbsp
Pinch of five spice powder			
Grated coconut cream	50 g	2 oz	4 tbsp
Chicken breast, cubed	225 g	8 oz	2 cups
Oil	30 ml	2 tbsp	2 tbsp
Finely chopped fresh root ginger	5 ml	1 tsp	1 tsp
Crushed garlic	5 ml	1 tsp	1 tsp
Finely chopped coriander (cilantro)	15 ml	1 tbsp	1 tbsp

1. Mix the curry powder and five spice powder in a cup with 30 ml/2 tbsp of cold water.

2. Put the grated coconut cream in a jug with 300 ml/ ½ pt/1¼ cups of hot water and stir to dissolve.

3. Marinate the cubed chicken with the curry paste mixture in a glass dish for about 15 minutes.

4. Heat the oil and stir-fry the ginger and garlic for 30 seconds. Add the chicken and marinade and stir-fry for 5 minutes.

5. Add the creamed coconut and water mixture and stir. Cook uncovered for 15 minutes or until the liquid is reduced.

6. Finally, add the coriander.

Preparation time: 7 minutes, plus 15 minutes marinating
Cooking time: 20 –25 minutes

GARLIC CHICKEN

Serves 2	Metric	Imperial	American
Egg white	1	1	1
Salt	2.5 ml	½ tsp	½ tsp
Cornflour (cornstarch)	30 ml	2 tbsp	2 tbsp
Chicken breast, thinly sliced	225 g	8 oz	2 cups
Stock or water	85 ml	3 fl oz	5½ tbsp
Sweet chilli sauce	15 ml	1 tbsp	1 tbsp
Light soy sauce	10 ml	2 tsp	2 tsp
Sugar	10 ml	2 tsp	2 tsp
Cornflour (cornstarch)	5 ml	1 tsp	1 tsp
Oil	30 ml	2 tbsp	2 tbsp
Crushed garlic	20 ml	4 tsp	4 tsp
Mangetout (snow peas)	50 g	2 oz	2 oz

1. Mix together the egg white, salt and the 30 ml/2 tbsp of cornflour. Add the chicken and marinate for 15 minutes.

2. Mix together the stock or water, chilli sauce, soy sauce, sugar and the 5 ml/1 tsp of cornflour.

3. Heat the oil and stir-fry the garlic for 30 seconds.

4. Remove the chicken from the marinade and add to the hot oil. Stir-fry for about 3 minutes until light golden.

5. Add the mangetout peas and stir-fry for 3 minutes.

6. Finally, add the mixed sauce ingredients and stir until thickened slightly.

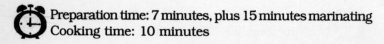

Preparation time: 7 minutes, plus 15 minutes marinating
Cooking time: 10 minutes

Garlic Beef

Follow the recipe for Garlic Chicken but substitute 225 g/ 8 oz/2 cups of thinly sliced raw beef for the chicken.

Garlic Pork

Follow the recipe for Garlic Chicken but substitute 225 g/ 8 oz/2 cups of thinly sliced raw pork for the chicken.

Garlic Prawns

Follow the recipe for Garlic Chicken but substitute 225 g/ 8 oz/2 cups of raw prawns (shrimp) for the chicken.

CHINESE MEATBALLS

Serves 2	Metric	Imperial	American
Minced (ground) beef	225 g	8 oz	2 cups
Crushed fresh root ginger	2.5 ml	½ tsp	½ tsp
Crushed garlic	2.5 ml	½ tsp	½ tsp
Pinch of five spice powder			
Curry Sauce (page 25) 1 recipe			
Tomato purée (paste)	10 ml	2 tsp	2 tsp
Stock	50 ml	2 fl oz	3½ tbsp

1. Put the mince, ginger, garlic and five spice powder in a bowl and knead well with one hand. Leave for 10 minutes, then shape into 8-10 balls.

2. Make up the Curry Sauce and add the tomato purée and additional stock.

3. Bring the sauce to the boil, then carefully drop in the meatballs. Cook over moderate heat for about 30 minutes until the sauce has thickened and the meatballs are cooked.

 Preparation time: 10 minutes, plus 10 minutes resting
Cooking time: 30–35 minutes

Braised Dishes

There is more to Chinese food than stir-frying. This selection of dishes shows how you can combine chicken, beef or pork with a tasty sauce and cook it slowly in a covered pan. The result is a succulent dish with a wonderful medley of flavours.

BRAISED CHICKEN

Serves 2	Metric	Imperial	American
Chicken breast, thickly sliced	225 g	8 oz	2 cups
Black bean sauce	15 ml	1 tbsp	1 tbsp
Honey	30 ml	2 tbsp	2 tbsp
Sherry	30 ml	2 tbsp	2 tbsp
Light soy sauce	30 ml	2 tbsp	2 tbsp
Dark soy sauce	15 ml	1 tbsp	1 tbsp
Crushed garlic	5 ml	1 tsp	1 tsp
Crushed fresh root ginger	5 ml	1 tsp	1 tsp
Oil	30 ml	2 tbsp	2 tbsp

1. Place all the ingredients except the oil in a bowl and marinate the chicken for about 30 minutes.

2. Heat the oil and stir-fry the chicken and its marinade until the chicken is sealed.

3. Add 150 ml/^{1}/$_4$ pt/^{2}/$_3$ cup of water. Cover the pan and simmer over low heat for about 30 minutes until the chicken is tender. This dish can be reheated.

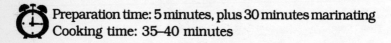 Preparation time: 5 minutes, plus 30 minutes marinating
Cooking time: 35–40 minutes

Braised Beef

Follow the recipe for Braised Chicken but substitute 225 g/8 oz/2 cups of cubed Precooked Beef (page 24) for the chicken.

Braised Pork

Follow the recipe for Braised Chicken but substitute 225 g/8 oz/2 cups of raw cubed pork for the chicken, and add 15 ml/1 tbsp of sweet chilli sauce at step 2.

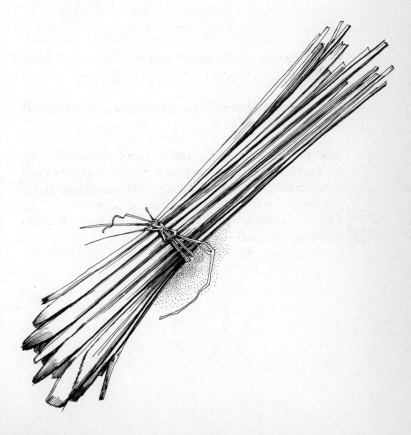

SLOW-COOKED CHICKEN

Serves 2	Metric	Imperial	American
Oil	30 ml	2 tbsp	2 tbsp
Chicken breast, cubed	225 g	8 oz	2 cups
Roughly chopped spring onion (scallion)	30 ml	2 tbsp	2 tbsp
Dried Chinese mushrooms, reconstituted and halved	4	4	4
Oyster sauce	30 ml	2 tbsp	2 tbsp
Dark soy sauce	15 ml	1 tbsp	1 tbsp
Sweet chilli sauce	15 ml	1 tbsp	1 tbsp
Sugar	15 ml	1 tbsp	1 tbsp

1. Heat the oil, add the chicken and stir-fry for 3 minutes until sealed.

2. Add the spring onion and mushrooms and stir-fry for 30 seconds.

3. Add the remaining ingredients plus 150 ml/$^1/_4$ pt/ $^2/_3$ cup of water and stir well. Cover the pan and simmer over low heat for about 30 minutes until the chicken is tender. This dish can be reheated.

Preparation time: 7 minutes
Cooking time: 35–40 minutes

Slow-cooked Beef

Follow the recipe for Slow-cooked Chicken but substitute 225 g/8 oz/2 cups of cubed Precooked Beef (page 24) for the chicken, and add 1 whole star anise at step 2.

Slow-cooked Pork

Follow the recipe for Slow-cooked Chicken but substitute 225 g/8 oz/2 cups of cubed raw pork for the chicken.

SLOW-COOKED ORANGE CHICKEN

Serves 2	Metric	Imperial	American
Oil	30 ml	2 tbsp	2 tbsp
Crushed garlic	10 ml	2 tsp	2 tsp
Crushed fresh root ginger	10 ml	2 tsp	2 tsp
Chicken breast, cut into large chunks	225 g	8 oz	2 cups
Orange, zest and juice only	1	1	1
Chopped spring onion (scallion)	15 ml	1 tbsp	1 tbsp
Sugar	10 ml	2 tsp	2 tsp
Light Sauce (page 19, omitting the cornflour/ cornstarch) 1 recipe			
Lemon sauce	30 ml	2 tbsp	2 tbsp

1. Heat the oil, add the garlic and ginger and stir-fry for 30 seconds.

2. Add the chicken and stir-fry until golden. Add the orange zest and juice, spring onion, sugar, sauce and lemon sauce. Reduce the heat to very low and cook, covered, for 30 minutes. This dish can be reheated.

 Preparation time: 5 minutes
Cooking time: 35–40 minutes

Slow-cooked Orange Beef

Follow the recipe for Slow-cooked Orange Chicken but substitute 225 g/8 oz/2 cups of cubed Precooked Beef (page 24) for the chicken.

Slow-cooked Orange Pork

Follow the recipe for Slow-cooked Orange Chicken but substitute 225 g/8 oz/2 cups of cubed raw pork for the chicken.

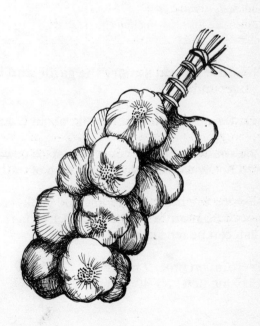

SLOW-COOKED GINGER CHICKEN

Serves 2	Metric	Imperial	American
Oil	30 ml	2 tbsp	2 tbsp
Crushed garlic	10 ml	2 tsp	2 tsp
Finely chopped fresh root ginger	15 ml	1 tbsp	1 tbsp
Chicken breast or portions, cut into bite-sized pieces	225 g	8 oz	2 cups
Light Sauce (page 19, omitting the cornflour/ cornstarch) 1 recipe			
Honey	15 ml	1 tbsp	1 tbsp
Pinch of five spice powder			
Ginger and honey spare rib sauce	15 ml	1 tbsp	1 tbsp

1. Heat the oil and stir-fry the garlic and ginger for 30 seconds.

2. Add the chicken and stir-fry for about 5 minutes.

3. Add the Light Sauce, honey, five spice powder, ginger and honey sauce and 15 ml/1 tbsp of water.

4. Reduce the heat to very low and cook, covered, for about 30 minutes until the chicken is tender. This dish can be reheated.

Preparation time: 7 minutes
Cooking time: 35–40 minutes

Slow-cooked Ginger Beef

Follow the recipe for Slow-cooked Ginger Chicken but substitute 225 g/8 oz/2 cups of cubed Precooked Beef (page 24) for the chicken.

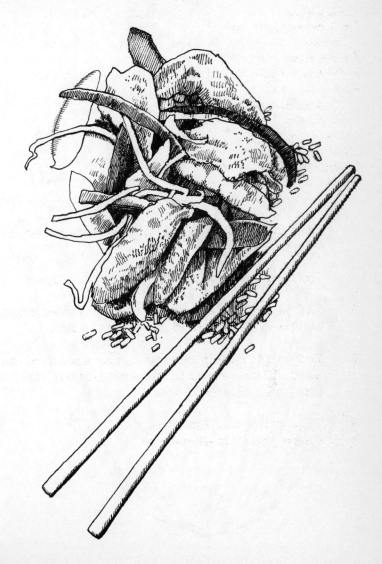

VEGETABLE & VEGETARIAN Dishes

Just because meat is excluded from your diet doesn't mean you have to miss out on Chinese food. The same cooking methods can be just as successful when applied to vegetables. Combine them with traditional Chinese ingredients and seasonings and you will produce that unmistakable Oriental flavour.

BROCCOLI IN SAUCE

Serves 2	Metric	Imperial	American
Oil	*30 ml*	*2 tbsp*	*2 tbsp*
Crushed garlic	*5 ml*	*1 tsp*	*1 tsp*
Crushed fresh root ginger	*5 ml*	*1 tsp*	*1 tsp*
Broccoli florets, blanched	*225 g*	*8 oz*	*2 cups*
Sugar	*10 ml*	*2 tsp*	*2 tsp*
Cornflour (cornstarch)	*5 ml*	*1 tsp*	*1 tsp*
Sesame seeds	*5 ml*	*1 tsp*	*1 tsp*

1. Heat the oil and stir-fry the garlic and ginger for 30 seconds.

2. Add the broccoli and stir-fry for 2 minutes. Add all the remaining ingredients plus 50 ml/2 fl oz/3¹/₂ tbsp of cold water. Stir-fry for about 1 minute until the sauce has thickened slightly.

 Preparation time: 7 minutes
Cooking time: 5 minutes

VEGETABLES WITH EGG

Serves 2	Metric	Imperial	American
Oil	30 ml	2 tbsp	2 tbsp
Lettuce, halved and thinly sliced	100 g	4 oz	1 cup
Dried Chinese mushrooms, reconstituted and sliced	4	4	4
Carrot, sliced and blanched	1	1	1
Chopped spring onion (scallion)	30 ml	2 tbsp	2 tbsp
Crushed garlic	5 ml	1 tsp	1 tsp
Crushed fresh root ginger	5 ml	1 tsp	1 tsp
Sugar	10 ml	2 tsp	2 tsp
Light soy sauce	10 ml	2 tsp	2 tsp
Eggs, beaten	3	3	3

1. Heat the oil and add all the vegetables, garlic and ginger. Stir-fry for 3 minutes.

2. Add the sugar, soy sauce and eggs and stir-fry until the eggs are just scrambled and mixed with the other ingredients.

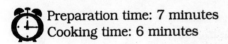 Preparation time: 7 minutes
Cooking time: 6 minutes

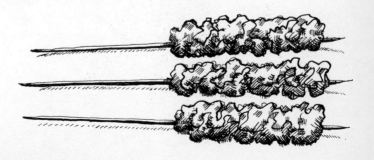

STIR-FRIED MIXED VEGETABLES

Serves 2	Metric	Imperial	American
Oil	30 ml	2 tbsp	2 tbsp
Crushed garlic	5 ml	1 tsp	1 tsp
Crushed fresh root ginger	5 ml	1 tsp	1 tsp
Carrot, sliced and blanched	1	1	1
Red (bell) pepper, sliced	½	½	½
Chopped spring onion (scallion)	30 ml	2 tbsp	2 tbsp
Lettuce, sliced	½	½	½
Bean sprouts	100 g	4 oz	1 cup
Sesame seeds	5 ml	1 tsp	1 tsp
Oyster sauce	15 ml	1 tbsp	1 tbsp
Sweet chilli sauce	15 ml	1 tbsp	1 tbsp

1. Heat the oil and stir-fry the garlic and ginger for 30 seconds.

2. Add the carrot, red pepper, spring onion and lettuce and stir-fry for 2 minutes.

3. Add the remaining ingredients and stir-fry for 2 minutes.

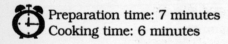 Preparation time: 7 minutes
Cooking time: 6 minutes

MIXED VEGETABLES

Serves 2	Metric	Imperial	American
Oil	30 ml	2 tbsp	2 tbsp
Sesame oil	5 ml	1 tsp	1 tsp
Red (bell) pepper, cut into triangles	50 g	2 oz	1 cup
Green beans, halved	50 g	2 oz	1/2 cup
Button mushrooms, halved	50 g	2 oz	1 cup
Dried Chinese mushrooms, reconstituted and quartered	4	4	4
Sliced carrot, blanched	25 g	1 oz	1 tbsp
Small broccoli florets, blanched	50 g	2 oz	1 cup
Bean sprouts	50 g	2 oz	1/2 cup
Light Sauce (page 19) 1 recipe			

1. Heat the oils and stir-fry the red pepper, green beans, button mushrooms, Chinese mushrooms and carrot for 2 minutes.

2. Add the broccoli, bean sprouts and Light Sauce and cook until thickened slightly.

 Preparation time: 8–10 minutes
Cooking time: 6–10 minutes

SPECIAL VEGETARIAN SPRING ROLLS

Serves 2	Metric	Imperial	American
Spring roll wrappers	8	8	8
For the filling			
Oil	30 ml	2 tbsp	2 tbsp
Finely chopped fresh root ginger	5 ml	1 tsp	1 tsp
Crushed garlic	5 ml	1 tsp	1 tsp
Grated celery	25 g	1 oz	2 tbsp
Finely grated carrot	25 g	1 oz	2 tbsp
Dried Chinese mushrooms, reconstituted and finely chopped	5	5	5
Dark soy sauce	5 ml	1 tsp	1 tsp
Light soy sauce	5 ml	1 tsp	1 tsp
Sesame oil	5 ml	1 tsp	1 tsp
Sugar	5 ml	1 tsp	1 tsp
Pinch of five spice powder			
Bean sprouts	50 g	2 oz	1/2 cup
Spring onions (scallions), finely chopped	2	2	2
Cornflour (cornstarch)	5 ml	1 tsp	1 tsp
For the paste			
Plain (all-purpose) flour	15 ml	1 tbsp	1 tbsp

1. To make the filling, heat the oil and stir-fry the ginger and garlic for 30 seconds.

2. Add the celery, carrots and mushrooms and stir-fry for 1 minute.

3. Add the soy sauces, sesame oil, sugar and five spice powder and stir-fry for 30 seconds.

4. Add the bean sprouts, spring onions and the cornflour mixed with 5 ml/1 tsp of cold water. Stir-fry until the liquid is reduced. Allow to go cold before using.

5. To make the paste, mix the flour with 15 ml/1 tbsp of cold water.

6. To fill the rolls, place about 25 g/1 oz of the filling in a strip 5 cm (2 in) in from each side and the base of the wrapper. Fold the unfilled piece at the base over to cover the filling. Fold the unfilled right side over the filling towards the left and the unfilled left side over the filling towards the right. Now roll up tightly and seal the join of the roll with the flour and water paste. (See diagram on page 33.)

7. Deep-fry the prepared spring rolls in oil heated to 180°C/350°F for about 5 minutes until golden brown.

Preparation time: 5 minutes
Cooking time: 5 minutes

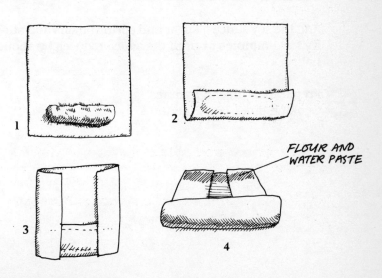

FLOUR AND WATER PASTE

MUSHROOMS

Serves 2	Metric	Imperial	American
Oil	15 ml	1 tbsp	1 tbsp
Crushed garlic	10 ml	2 tsp	2 tsp
Crushed fresh root ginger	10 ml	2 tsp	2 tsp
Button mushrooms, halved	175 g	6 oz	3 cups
Dried Chinese mushrooms, reconstituted and halved	4	4	4
Dark soy sauce	30 ml	2 tbsp	2 tbsp
Light soy sauce	15 ml	1 tbsp	1 tbsp
Sugar	10 ml	2 tsp	2 tsp
Spring onions (scallions), finely chopped	2	2	2

1. Heat the oil and stir-fry the garlic and ginger for 30 seconds.

2. Add the button mushrooms and Chinese mushrooms and stir-fry for 5 minutes.

3. Add the soy sauces, sugar and spring onions and stir-fry for 4 minutes or until the sauce reduces by about half.

 Preparation time: 5 minutes
Cooking time: 10–12 minutes

SPICY MUSHROOMS

Serves 2	Metric	Imperial	American
Oil	15 ml	1 tbsp	1 tbsp
Crushed garlic	5 ml	1 tsp	1 tsp
Crushed fresh root ginger	5 ml	1 tsp	1 tsp
Whole button mushrooms	175 g	6 oz	3 cups
Dried Chinese mushrooms, reconstituted and left whole	4	4	4
Sweet chilli sauce	10 ml	2 tsp	2 tsp
Light soy sauce	5 ml	1 tsp	1 tsp
Dark soy sauce	5 ml	1 tsp	1 tsp
Sugar	5 ml	1 tsp	1 tsp

1. Heat the oil, add the garlic and ginger and stir-fry for 30 seconds.

2. Add the button and Chinese mushrooms and stir-fry for 2 minutes.

3. Add all the remaining ingredients plus 15 ml/1 tbsp of water and stir-fry until the sauce has almost disappeared.

Preparation time: 5 minutes
Cooking time: 5–8 minutes

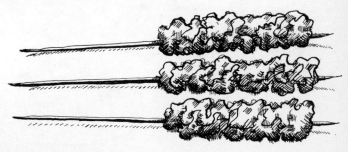

MUSHROOMS IN SOY SAUCE

Serves 2	Metric	Imperial	American
Whole button mushrooms	*225 g*	*8 oz*	*4 cups*
Light soy sauce	*10 ml*	*2 tsp*	*2 tsp*
Dark soy sauce	*10 ml*	*2 tsp*	*2 tsp*
Sugar	*10 ml*	*2 tsp*	*2 tsp*
Sesame oil	*5 ml*	*1 tsp*	*1 tsp*

Place all the ingredients plus 15 ml/1 tbsp of water in a saucepan and stir-fry until the liquid has almost disappeared and the mushrooms are coated thoroughly.

 Preparation/cooking time: 5–8 minutes

BROCCOLI STIR-FRY

Serves 2	Metric	Imperial	American
Cornflour (cornstarch)	*5 ml*	*1 tsp*	*1 tsp*
Yellow bean sauce	*15 ml*	*1 tbsp*	*1 tbsp*
Sweet chilli sauce	*10 ml*	*2 tsp*	*2 tsp*
Light soy sauce	*15 ml*	*1 tbsp*	*1 tbsp*
Oil	*30 ml*	*2 tbsp*	*2 tbsp*
Crushed garlic	*5 ml*	*1 tsp*	*1 tsp*
Crushed fresh root ginger	*5 ml*	*1 tsp*	*1 tsp*
Broccoli, separated into florets	*100 g*	*4 oz*	*1 cup*
Bamboo shoots	*50 g*	*2 oz*	*1/2 cup*
Sliced celery	*50 g*	*2 oz*	*1/2 cup*

1. Mix the cornflour with 15 ml/1 tbsp of cold water and add the yellow bean sauce, chilli sauce and the light soy sauce. Mix together.

2. Heat the oil and stir-fry the garlic and ginger for 30 seconds.

3. Add the vegetables and stir-fry for 3-5 minutes.

4. Add the sauce mixture and stir-fry until the vegetables are coated and the sauce slightly thickened.

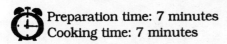
Preparation time: 7 minutes
Cooking time: 7 minutes

VEGETABLES IN BLACK BEAN SAUCE

Serves 2	Metric	Imperial	American
Light soy sauce	15 ml	1 tbsp	1 tbsp
Black bean sauce	5 ml	1 tsp	1 tsp
Cornflour (cornstarch)	5 ml	1 tsp	1 tsp
Oil	30 ml	2 tbsp	2 tbsp
Green beans, halved and blanched	100 g	4 oz	1 cup
Roughly chopped onion	50 g	2 oz	1/2 cup
Tinned straw mushrooms	100 g	4 oz	1 cup
Thinly sliced carrots, blanched	50 g	2 oz	1/2 cup

1. Mix together the soy sauce, black bean sauce, cornflour and 15 ml/1 tbsp of cold water.

2. Heat the oil and stir-fry all the vegetables for 3 minutes.

3. Finally, add the sauce mix and stir-fry to coat the vegetables and until the sauce has thickened slightly.

 Preparation time: 7 minutes
Cooking time: 6 minutes

STIR-FRIED LETTUCE IN CHILLI SAUCE

Serves 2	Metric	Imperial	American
Oil	30 ml	2 tbsp	2 tbsp
Crushed garlic	5 ml	1 tsp	1 tsp
Crushed fresh root ginger	5 ml	1 tsp	1 tsp
Dried Chinese mushrooms, reconstituted and sliced	6	6	6
Lettuce, halved and cut into thick slices	1	1	1
Sugar	5 ml	1 tsp	1 tsp
Sweet chilli sauce	5 ml	1 tsp	1 tsp
Light soy sauce	5 ml	1 tsp	1 tsp

1. Heat the oil and stir-fry the garlic and ginger for 30 seconds.

2. Add the mushrooms and stir-fry for 3 minutes. Add the lettuce and stir-fry for 1 minute.

3. Finally, add the sugar, chilli sauce and soy sauce and stir-fry until the vegetables are well coated.

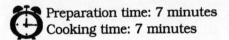
Preparation time: 7 minutes
Cooking time: 7 minutes

DESSERTS

A good pudding is the only way to round off a Chinese meal, whether it is in a restaurant, from a take-away, or one you have cooked at home. Indulge yourself!

CHINESE RICE PUDDING

Serves 2	Metric	Imperial	American
Pudding rice	50 g	2 oz	¼ cup
Salt	5 ml	1 tsp	1 tsp
Full cream milk	1.2 litres	2 pts	5 cups
Granulated sugar	150 g	5 oz	²/₃ cup
Few drops of vanilla essence (extract)			
Pinch of ground cinnamon			

1. Place the rice in a saucepan and pour in plenty of water. With one hand agitate the rice until the water turns cloudy, then discard as much water as possible. Repeat this process two or three times until the water no longer goes cloudy. Drain the rice thoroughly through a sieve and return to the saucepan.

2. Pour in enough water to cover the rice plus about 1 cm/ ½ in. Add the salt and allow to stand for about 40 minutes.

3. Bring to the boil and continue boiling, uncovered, until the liquid evaporates completely. Stir the rice a couple of times to distribute it in the pan. Switch off the heat, cover the pan and leave for about 5-10 minutes to fluff up.

4. Pour the milk into the cooked rice and bring it just to the boil.

5.   Add the sugar, vanilla essence and ground cinnamon. Simmer over gentle heat for about 1 hour until the milk has thickened and no longer looks watery. Serve hot, or chill well.

 Preparation time: 5 minutes, plus 40 minutes standing
Cooking time: 1 hour 20 minutes, plus optional chilling

SWEET WONTONS

Serves 2	Metric	Imperial	American
Wonton wrappers, bought or home-made (page 15)	8	8	8
Oil for shallow frying			
For the filling			
Ground almonds	50 g	2 oz	4 tbsp
Pinch of ground cinnamon			
Caster (superfine) sugar	25 g	1 oz	2 tbsp
Grated lemon zest	5 ml	1 tsp	1 tsp
Top of the milk or single (light) cream	5 ml	1 tsp	1 tsp
For the lemon syrup			
Granulated sugar	100 g	4 oz	½ cup
Lemon, juice only	1	1	1
For the coating			
Sesame seeds, lightly toasted	30 ml	2 tbsp	2 tbsp

1. Mix together all the filling ingredients.

2. Place about 5 ml/1 tsp of the filling mixture on each wonton. With your finger, wet the edges of each wonton and then fold them over to make a triangle shape. Seal really well by pressing down all along the sealed edge with the tines of a fork.

3. Heat about 2.5 cm/1 in of oil in a frying pan (skillet) and fry (sauté) the stuffed wontons for about 3 minutes until golden. Remove and place on kitchen paper to drain.

4. To make the lemon syrup, mix together the sugar and lemon juice in a pan with 120 ml/4 fl oz/½ cup of water. Bring to the boil and boil for 4 minutes. Remove from the heat.

5. Dip the stuffed fried wontons in the syrup to coat completely. Drain off excess syrup, dip in the sesame seeds, and place on a plate until cold.

You could serve the wontons dusted with icing (confectioners') sugar instead of the lemon syrup and sesame seed coating.

Preparation time: 10 minutes
Cooking time: 7 minutes, plus finishing

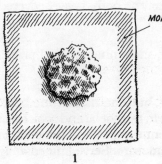

MOISTEN

1

2

BANANA FRITTERS

Serves 2	Metric	Imperial	American
Plain (all-purpose) flour	50 g	2 oz	½ cup
Pinch of salt			
Egg, size 2	1	1	1
Milk and water mixed	50 ml	2 fl oz	3½ tbsp
Oil for deep frying			
Caster (superfine) sugar	25 g	1 oz	2 tbsp
Ground cinnamon	5 ml	1 tsp	1 tsp
Bananas, cut in half			
lengthways	2	2	2

1. Put the flour, salt and egg in a bowl with half the liquid. Mix together, then slowly add the rest of the liquid. Beat well until completely smooth. Leave, covered, for about 15 minutes.

2. Mix together the sugar and cinnamon and place on a plate.

3. Heat the oil. Dip each banana half in the batter to cover completely. Place in the hot oil and cook for about 3 minutes. Remove from the pan and roll each in the sugar and cinnamon mixture. Serve immediately.

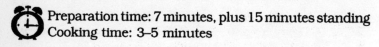 Preparation time: 7 minutes, plus 15 minutes standing
Cooking time: 3–5 minutes

Pineapple Fritters

Follow the recipe for Banana Fritters but use four tinned pineapple rings instead of the bananas.

CHINESE LEMON AND COCONUT TART

Serves 2	Metric	Imperial	American
Plain (all-purpose) flour	100 g	4 oz	1 cup
Block margarine, softened	50 g	2 oz	1/4 cup
Caster (superfine) sugar	10 ml	2 tsp	2 tsp
Pinch of salt			
Jar of lemon curd	1	1	1
Sweetened desiccated (shredded) coconut	30 ml	2 tbsp	2 tbsp

1. Put the flour in a bowl and rub in the margarine until it resembles fine breadcrumbs. Add the sugar and salt and then just enough water (about 15-30 ml/1-2 tbsp) to bind the ingredients together.

2. Preheat the oven to 190°C/375°F/gas mark 5. Roll out the pastry (paste), not too thinly, to line an 18 cm/7 in sandwich tin. Prick the base and sides thoroughly with a fork, then bake blind for about 15-20 minutes.

3. Carefully take the baked pastry from the tin and place on a serving plate. Fill with the lemon curd and even it out, and sprinkle over the coconut. Serve cut in slices.

Preparation time: 8 minutes
Cooking time: 20 minutes, plus finishing

Chinese Orange and Coconut Tart

Follow the recipe for Chinese Lemon and Coconut Tart but substitute a jar of orange curd for the lemon curd.

CHINESE COCONUT CAKE

Serves 2	Metric	Imperial	American
Eggs, size 2	2	2	2
Lemon or orange, zest only	1	1	1
Lemon or orange essence (extract)	2.5 ml	½ tsp	½ tsp
Pinch of salt			
Sugar	225 g	8 oz	1 cup
Plain (all-purpose) flour	225 g	8 oz	2 cups
Baking powder	10 ml	2 tsp	2 tsp
Whipping cream, whipped to soft peak stage	200 ml	7 fl oz	scant 1 cup
Apricot jam (conserve)	60 ml	4 tbsp	4 tbsp
Desiccated (shredded) coconut	60 ml	4 tbsp	4 tbsp

1. Grease and base line two 20-23 cm/8-9 in sandwich tins. Preheat the oven to 160°C/325°F/gas mark 3.

2. Using an electric whisk, beat the eggs until light and fluffy. Add the zest and essence, then the salt. Gradually add the sugar, beating well until the mixture thickens slightly.

3. Sift together the flour and baking powder, then sift half the flour over the egg mix and fold in. Then fold in half the whipped cream. Repeat with the remaining flour and cream.

4. Divide the mixture between the tins and bake in the centre of the oven for about 1 hour. When cooked, remove from the oven, cool in the tin for 5 minutes, then place on a wire rack to go completely cold.

5.   Spread the top of each cake with half the apricot jam
      and sprinkle over the desiccated coconut.

 Preparation time: 15 minutes
Cooking time: 1 hour, plus finishing

Apricot and Marzipan

Cover the top and sides of the Chinese Coconut Cake with
melted apricot jam, then roll out 100 g/4 oz of marzipan
(almond paste) into two circles, one to fit each cake. Cover the
cakes with the marzipan and then cut into triangles.

Raspberry and Coconut

Cut the Chinese Coconut Cake into 8 triangles before
coating at step 4. Heat 60 ml/4 tbsp of raspberry jam
(conserve) and dip each triangle in the jam to coat just the
top and sides. Then dip in 90 ml/6 tbsp of desiccated
coconut.

Cinnamon and Ginger

Follow the recipe for Chinese Coconut Cake, but substitute
5 ml/1 tsp of ground cinnamon and 25 g/1 oz/2 tbsp of finely
chopped preserved ginger for the lemon or orange zest and
essence.

CHINESE CUSTARD TARTS

Serves 2	Metric	Imperial	American
Plain (all purpose) flour	225 g	8 oz	2 cups
Pinch of salt			
Block margarine, softened	100 g	4 oz	½ cup
Caster (superfine) sugar	15 ml	1 tbsp	1 tbsp
For the filling			
Custard powder	30 ml	2 tbsp	2 tbsp
Caster (superfine) sugar	30 ml	2 tbsp	2 tbsp
Milk	600 ml	1 pt	2½ cups
Desiccated (shredded) coconut or toasted sesame seeds (optional)			

1. Preheat the oven to 190°C/375°F/gas mark 5.

2. Put the flour and salt in a bowl and rub in the margarine until it resembles fine breadcrumbs. Add the sugar and enough water (about 60-90 ml/4-6 tbsp) to bind the ingredients together.

3. Roll out the pastry (paste), not too thinly, then cut out enough circles to line approximately 12 patty tins. Prick well with a fork and bake for about 20 minutes until golden. Remove from the oven and cool.

4. Make up the custard according to the packet instructions. Wait until it is almost cold, then spoon into the individual pastry cases. Allow to set. Serve when completely cold, either plain or sprinkled with desiccated coconut or toasted sesame seeds.

Preparation time : 12 minutes
Cooking time: 25 minutes, plus cooling and finishing

MENU
SUGGESTIONS

Putting together a selection of dishes to create a complete menu is part of the enjoyment of cooking. However, if you are unsure which flavours and textures go well together some suggested menus are given here to point you in the right direction. Use them as they stand or adapt them to suit your own taste.

SUGGESTIONS FOR TWO

a. Spring Rolls (2), Beef with Mushrooms, Slow-cooked Chicken, Plain Fried Rice, Prawn Crackers, Chinese Custard Tarts (2)

b. Peking-style Spare Ribs, Chicken with Mushrooms, Slow-cooked Beef, Plain Boiled Rice, Pineapple Fritters (2)

c. Chilli Spare Ribs, Beef with Cashew Nuts, Slow-cooked Orange Chicken, Plain Boiled Rice, Chinese Rice Pudding

d. Barbecued Spare Ribs, Pork with Peppers and Black Bean Sauce, Slow-cooked Orange Beef, Plain Fried Rice, Sweet Wontons (4)

e. Deep-fried Wontons with Sweet and Sour Sauce, Chicken and Mushroom Soup, Beef Satay, Fried Noodles, Chinese Lemon and Coconut Tart

f. Prawn Toast, Special Beef Spring Rolls, Chicken Satay, Prawn Crackers, Egg Fried Rice, Banana Fritters (2)

g. Marbled Tea Eggs, Chinese Triangles, Slow-cooked Chicken, Plain Boiled Rice, Chinese Coconut Cake (2)

h. Prawn-stuffed Mushrooms, Barbecued Spare Ribs, Garlic Chicken, Fried Noodles, Chinese Orange and Coconut Tart

VEGETARIAN MENUS FOR TWO

a.   Marbled Tea Eggs (2), Spicy Mushrooms, Broccoli in Sauce, Plain Boiled Rice, Sweet Wontons.

b.   Vegetables with Egg, Sesame Fried Noodles, Spicy Mushrooms, Chinese Lemon & Coconut Tart (2 pieces)

c.   Mixed Vegetables, Marbled Tea Eggs (2), Plain Fried Rice, Mushrooms in Soy Sauce, Chinese Rice Pudding

d.   Mushrooms, Chips or Fried Noodles, Broccoli Stir-fry, Banana Fritters (2)

e.   Vegetables in Black Bean Sauce, Marbled Tea Eggs (2), Spicy Mushrooms, Fried Noodles, Chinese Coconut Cake (2 pieces)

f.   Stir-fried Mixed Vegetables, Plain Fried Rice, Spicy Mushrooms, Pineapple Fritters (2)

g.   Stir-fried Lettuce in Chilli Sauce, Mushrooms, Plain Boiled Rice, Chinese Orange and Coconut Tart (2 pieces)

SUGGESTIONS FOR THREE

a.   Peking-style Spare Ribs, Spring Rolls (3), Chicken with
     Cashew Nuts, Spicy Mushrooms, Slow-cooked Beef,
     Prawn Fried Rice, Chinese Orange and Coconut Tart
     (3)

b.   Prawn-stuffed Mushrooms, Braised Beef, Chicken
     Chow Mein, Pork Satay, Special Fried Rice, Chinese
     Custard Tarts (3)

c.   Chilli Spare Ribs, Deep-fried Wontons with Sweet and
     Sour Sauce, West Lake Soup, Stir-fried Chicken with
     Onions, Slow-cooked Ginger Beef, Plain Boiled Rice,
     Chinese Coconut Cake

d.   Prawn Crackers, Chinese Meatballs, Pork with
     Vegetables, Stuffed Chinese Mushrooms, Slow-cooked
     Orange Chicken, Plain Fried Rice, Ice Cream

e.   Prawn Toast, Marbled Tea Eggs, Cantonese-style
     Chicken Fillet, Chinese Rissoles, Sweet and Sour
     Sauce, Beef Chow Mein, Sweet Wontons

f.   Chinese Triangles, Beef in Fragrant Lemon Sauce,
     Slow-cooked Ginger Chicken, Spicy Mushrooms, Fried
     Noodles, Prawn Crackers, Pineapple Fritters (3)

g.   Broccoli in Sauce, Special Chicken Spring Rolls, Beef
     and Pineapple with Celery, Chicken and Sweetcorn
     Soup, Special Fried Rice, Banana Fritters (3)

h.   Special Beef Spring Rolls, Chicken in Fragrant
     Lemon Sauce, Prawn Fried Rice, Spicy Mushrooms,
     Slow-cooked Ginger Beef, Prawn Crackers, Chinese
     Rice Pudding

VEGETARIAN MENUS FOR THREE

a.   Spicy Mushrooms, Vegetables with Egg, Broccoli in Sauce, Plain Boiled Rice, Chinese Rice Pudding

b.   Marbled Tea Eggs (3), Fried Noodles, Spicy Mushrooms, Chinese Lemon and Coconut Tart (3 pieces)

c.   Mushrooms, Broccoli Stir-fry, Plain Boiled Rice, Stir-fried Mixed Vegetables, Pineapple Fritters (3)

d.   Vegetables in Black Bean Sauce, Broccoli in Sauce, Sesame Fried Noodles, Sweet Wontons (3)

e.   Stir-fried Mixed Vegetables, Spicy Mushrooms, Stir-fried Lettuce in Chilli Sauce, Plain Boiled Rice, Stir-fried Rice, Banana Fritters or Ice Cream

f.   Vegetables in Black Bean Sauce, Mushrooms in Soy Sauce, Marbled Tea Eggs (3), Fried Noodles, Chinese Custard Tarts (3)

g.   Mushrooms in Soy Sauce, Vegetables in Black Bean Sauce, Marbled Tea Eggs (3), Fried Noodles, Pineapple Fritters (3)

SUGGESTIONS FOR FOUR

a. Marbled Tea Eggs, Hot and Sour Soup, Chicken with Mushrooms, Spicy Mushrooms, Prawn Chow Mein, Szechuan Beef, Chinese Rice Pudding or Ice Cream

b. Prawn-stuffed Mushrooms, Chicken and Sweetcorn Soup, Beef with Cashew Nuts, Chicken Chow Mein, Braised Chicken, Chinese Custard Tarts (4)

c. Spring Rolls (4), Pork with Peppers and Black Bean Sauce, Egg Fried Rice, Skewered Chicken, Slow-cooked Beef, Chinese Lemon and Coconut Tart

d. Barbecued Spare Ribs, Prawn Satay, Special Fried Rice, Special Pork Spring Rolls (4), Char Shiu, Banana Fritters (4)

e. Peking-style Spare Ribs, Chicken and Mushroom Soup, Stir-fried Chicken with Onions, Beef Fried Rice, Prawn Crackers, Chinese Rice Pudding

f. Deep-fried Wontons with Sweet and Sour Sauce, Slow-cooked Orange Pork, Plain Boiled Rice, Szechuan Chicken, Chinese Custard Tarts or Ice Cream

g. Chilli Spare Ribs, West Lake Soup, Cantonese-style Fillet Steak, Fried Noodles, Chicken in Paper, Braised Pork, Chinese Coconut Cake

h. Prawn Toast, Pork with Pineapple, Egg Fried Rice, Special Chicken Spring Rolls (4), Chinese Triangles, Chinese Meatballs, Pineapple Fritters (4)

VEGETARIAN MENUS FOR FOUR

a. Broccoli in Sauce, Marbled Tea Eggs (4), Spicy Mushrooms, Plain Fried Rice, Chinese Rice Pudding, Chinese Orange and Coconut Tart (4 pieces)

b. Spicy Mushrooms, Vegetables with Egg, Plain Boiled Rice, Pineapple Fritters (4), Chinese Custard Tarts (4)

c. Broccoli Stir-fry, Marbled Tea Eggs (4), Sesame Fried Noodles, Spicy Mushrooms, Mushrooms in Soy Sauce, Sweet Wontons (4), Ice Cream

d. Vegetables in Black Bean Sauce, Plain Fried Rice, Mixed Vegetables, Spicy Mushrooms, Marbled Tea Eggs (4), Chinese Coconut Cake (4 pieces)

e. Stir-fried Lettuce in Chilli Sauce, Broccoli in Sauce, Mushrooms, Plain Boiled Rice, Banana Fritters (4) with Ice Cream

f. Broccoli in Sauce, Vegetables with Egg, Fried Noodles, Spicy Mushrooms, Chinese Custard Tarts (4)

g. Mushrooms in Soy Sauce, Marbled Tea Eggs (4), Mixed Vegetables, Broccoli in Sauce, Plain Boiled Rice, Pineapple Fritters (4), with Ice Cream

Index